The Winter Repertory
Michael Feingold / General Editor

A Winter Repertory Special Edition:

the
winter repertory

Grease

A NEW 50'S ROCK 'N ROLL MUSICAL

MUSIC, BOOK AND LYRICS BY

Jim Jacobs and Warren Casey

INTRODUCTION: MICHAEL FEINGOLD

WINTER HOUSE LTD

NEW YORK

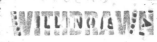

SYNOPSIS OF SCENES

Douglas W. Schmidt's set design for *Grease*
Over: The cast in Greased Lightning

INTRODUCTION

Goodbye to Sandra Dee

The 1950's have survived in the popular imagination as that decade when nothing happened. Yet in fact a great deal did: History does not stop simply because a fatherly ex-general is elected President of the United States. One thing that happened, for instance, was that the U.S. successfully prevented free elections, in direct contravention of the 1954 Geneva Accords, in a small Asian country, of which very few Americans had heard at the time. Thus, while the men who ran The Ed Sullivan Show were debating whether or not to show Elvis Presley's pelvic gyrations on national TV, America committed itself to the war in Vietnam.

Grease does not discourse about our presence in Saigon. Nor does it contain in-depth study of such other 50's developments as the growth of mega-corporations and conglomerates, the suburban building boom that broke the backs of our cities, the separation of labor's political power from the workers by union leaders and organization men. Although set in and around an urban high school, it does not even discuss one of the decade's dominant news stories, the massive expansion of the university system, and the directing of a whole generation of war babies toward the pursuit of college degrees. Grease is an escape, a musical designed to entertain, not to concern itself with serious political and social matters. But because it is truthful, because it spares neither the details nor the larger shapes of the narrow experience on which it focuses so tightly, Grease implies the topics I have raised, and many others. So I think it is a work of art, a firm image that projects, by means of what it does contain, everything it has chosen to leave out. And between the throbs of its ebullience, charm, and comedy, it conveys a feeling, about where we have been and how we got to where we are, that is quite near despair, if one wants to dwell on it.

Nostalgia is a pretty unhealthy emotion. In the theater it evades, more often than not, the reality of both past and present. It indulges ugly feelings of condescension toward the former ("Isn't that quaint!"), and of envy that comes from petty resentment of the latter ("They don't make shows like that anymore!"). *Grease*, however, does not evade; in that sense it is not a nostalgia show. One has to have some affectionate memory of a period one has outlived, and the musical does not scruple to show its affection for every person and thing involved; it is, I believe, utterly without hate. Yet it is objective about the triviality and emptiness of the lives it portrays, about the sweeping changes that have now rendered those lives obsolete, about the sweet manufactured insipidity of the music and lyrics that were a constant background to a 1950's adolescence.

The people of *Grease* are a special class of aliens, self-appointed cynics in a work-oriented, upwardly mobile world. We know from the prologue that history has played its dirty trick on them before they even appear: They are not at the reunion; they will not be found among the prosperous Mrs. Honeywells and the go-getting vice-presidents of Straight-Shooters, Unlimited. Nor, on the other hand, did they actively drop out: that was left to their younger siblings and cousins. (Memory of a line too explicit, and cut from the script early on: "Course I like life. Whaddaya think I am, a beatnik?") They were the group who thought they had, or chose to have, nowhere to go. They stayed in the monotonous work routine of the lower middle class, acquiring, if they were lucky, enough status to move to one of the more nondescript suburbs, and losing their strongest virtue—the group solidarity that had made them, in high school, a force to be reckoned with. It is appropriate that the finale of *Grease* celebrates that solidarity, with the saving of its heroine, and the reclamation of its hero, from the clutches of respectability—a good lusty razz at the sanctimonious endings of those Sal Mineo j.d. movies (*Somebody Up There Likes Me*, remember?) wherein the tough punk is saved for society at the end. Everybody knew you didn't go to those films to see that part.

Here, as elsewhere, *Grease* is in possession of a truth, one of its strongest, about the media and how they worked on us. This is of course best seen in its superb, sharp-eared songs. The musical basis of 50's rock is fractured by comedy quite early in the enumeration of "Those Magic Changes." After that it is a matter of astonishment how many delicate subforms there were to the songs of the period, and how many different comic approaches Jim Jacobs and Warren Casey use to pin them down: Imitative *hommage* ("Rock 'n Roll Party Queen"), outright burlesque ("Sandra Dee"), ironic, look-the-other-way dirty joke ("Mooning"), character satire ("Freddy, My Love"), improbable-situation parody ("Beauty School Dropout"), and, best of all to my taste, the quiet revelation of fact as an antidote to the sentimentality of the originals. Take "It's Raining on Prom Night":

> I don't even have my corsage, oh gee,
> It fell down a sewer with my sister's I.D.

Truthful, admittedly, but pretty squalid. Small. Petty. Not the deep sentimental tragedy you will find in a prototypical "serious" song like "Tell Tommy I Miss Him" or "Teen Angel." This song is easier to laugh at than some of the others because it is more firmly distanced —not a report of something that actually happens to our heroine, just a convenient index to her momentary emotions.

"There Are Worse Things I Could Do" seems a harder case, momentarily: What is this ostensibly serious, "dramatic" song doing in the middle of this rumbustious, frivolous show? But after all, it, too, is a parody. The seriousness of the situation is equalled only by its smallness: "Even though the neighborhood/Thinks I'm trashy and no good . . ." Here again the point is not sympathy, or dramatic urgency, but history: This feeling, now obsolete, was recorded during the 1950's. Make of it what you will. The greatest achievement of *Grease* (and the aspect which produces the loudest laughter in the packed house every night) is its perfect deadpan objectivity about everything in it: A d.a. haircut, a new guitar, a missed period, a falsetto backup group, a preposterously accurate hand-jive. It is a loving, funny, museum of where we were, perhaps even, when we scream and stomp our feet at it, a gentle attempt to exorcize the parts of ourselves we left back there, a tribute to the many small, stupid things that happened to us during "the decade when nothing happened." If, after we see it, after we have our hearty laugh and our tender glow at the memory of where we were, we scream silently, "How did we end up here?", or shudder at the memory of the greasers we left back there—if we do that, it is entirely up to us. The authors have left the case open, and the depths are there only if you want to dig for them—it's equally easy to have a good time and look no further. But we might as well face the fact that sooner or later we all have to say "goodbye to Sandra Dee," and to her cohorts in the field of illusion. *Grease* is a warm, laugh-loaded, relaxing way to get disillusioned, as honest in its comedy as any great musical of the 20's or 30's. So don't let anybody tell you they don't make shows like that anymore.

Michael Feingold

Left: Carrie F. Robbins' costume sketch
for Frenchy of The Pink Ladies
Above: The Pink Ladies
sing "Freddy, My Love," Act one

Grease was first performed in New York at the Eden Theatre on February 14, 1972. It was produced by Kenneth Waissman and Maxine Fox, in association with Anthony d'Amato, and directed by Tom Moore, with musical numbers and dances staged by Patricia Birch, scenery by Douglas W. Schmidt, costumes by Carrie F. Robbins, lighting by Karl Eigsti, orchestrations by Michael Leonard, musical direction and vocal arrangements by Louis St. Louis, and the following cast:

Miss Lynch	*Dorothy Leon*
Patty Simcox	*Ilene Kristen*
Eugene Florczyk	*Tom Harris*
Jan	*Garn Stephens*
Marty	*Katie Hanley*
Betty Rizzo	*Adrienne Barbeau*
Doody	*James Canning*
Roger	*Walter Bobbie*
Kenickie	*Timothy Meyers*
Sonny	*Jim Borrelli*
Frenchy	*Marya Small*
Sandy Dumbrowski	*Carole Demas*
Danny Zuko	*Barry Bostwick*
Vince Fontaine	*Don Billett*
Johnny Casino	*Alan Paul*
Cha-Cha Di Gregorio	*Kathi Moss*
Teen Angel	*Alan Paul*

This production transferred to the Broadhurst Theatre, New York, on June 7, 1972. *Grease* had previously been produced at the Kingston Mines Theater in Chicago in February, 1971.

Opposite: The Burger Palace Boys sing
"Greased Lightning," Act One   Over: Doody

REGULAR?
HOBBY JEA
LOAFERS
SNEAKERS
YES/BLK.

DANNY: The leader of the Burger Palace Boys. Well-built, nice-looking, with an air of cool, easygoing charm. Strong and confident.

SANDY: Danny's love interest. Sweet, wholesome, naive, cute, like Sandra Dee of the "Gidget" movies.

THE PINK LADIES, the club-jacketed, gum-chewing, hip-swinging girls' gang that hangs around with the Burger Palace Boys—

RIZZO: Leader of the Pink Ladies. She is tough, sarcastic and outspoken, but vulnerable. Thin, Italian, with unconventional good looks.

FRENCHY: A dreamer. Good-natured and dumb. Heavily made-up, fussy about her appearance—particularly her hair. She can't wait to finish high school so she can be a beautician.

MARTY: The "beauty" of the Pink Ladies. Pretty, looks older than the other girls, but betrays her real age when she opens her mouth. Tries to act sophisticated.

JAN: Chubby, compulsive eater. Loud and pushy with the girls, but shy with boys.

THE BURGER PALACE BOYS, A super-cool, d.a.-haired, hard-looking group of high school wheeler-dealers . . . or so they think—

KENICKIE: Second in command of the Burger Palace Boys. Tough-looking, tattooed, surly, avoids any show of softness. Has an offbeat sense of humor.

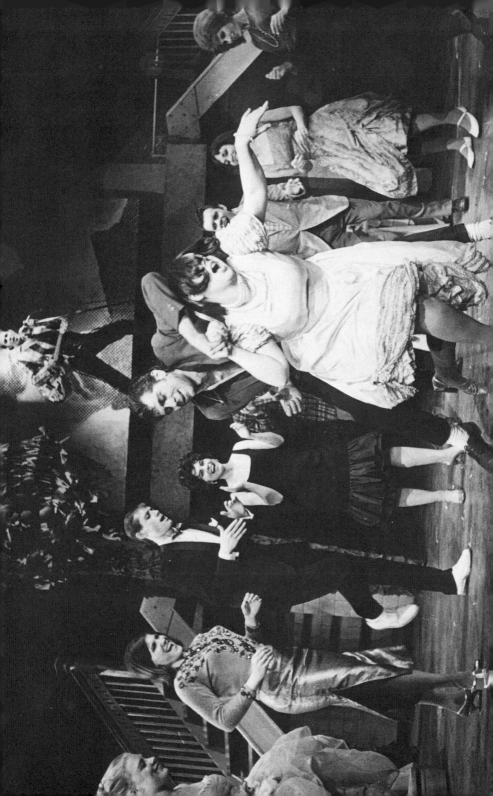

DOODY: Youngest of the guys. Small, boyish, open, with a disarming smile and a hero-worshipping attitude toward the others. Plays the guitar.

ROGER: The "anything-for-a-laugh" stocky type. Full of mischief, half-baked schemes and ideas. A clown who enjoys putting other people on.

SONNY: Italian-looking, with shiny black hair and dark oily skin. A braggart and wheeler-dealer who thinks he's a real lady-killer.

PATTY: A typical cheerleader at a middle-class American public high school. Attractive and athletic. Aggressive, sure of herself, given to bursts of disconcerting enthusiasm. Catty, but in an All-American-Girl sort of way. She can twirl a baton.

CHA-CHA: A blind date. Slovenly, loudmouthed and homely. Takes pride in being "the best dancer at St. Bernadette's."

EUGENE: The class valedictorian. Physically awkward, with weak eyes and a high-pitched voice. An apple-polisher, smug and pompous but gullible.

VINCE FONTAINE: A typical "teen audience" radio disc jockey. Slick, egotistical, fast-talking. A veteran "greaser."

JOHNNY CASINO: A "greaser" student at Rydell who leads a rock 'n roll band and likes to think of himself as a real rock 'n roll idol.

TEEN ANGEL: A good-looking, falsetto-voiced, Fabian look-alike. A singer who would have caused girls to scream and riot back in 1958.

MISS LYNCH: An old-maid English teacher.

Opposite: Cha-Cha and Danny
in the dance competition, Act two

ACT I / SCENE 1

Lights come up on the singing of the Rydell Alma Mater. Enter three people: MISS LYNCH, *an old maid English teacher who leads the singing;* PATTY, *former high school cheerleader and honor student, now a professional married career woman; and* EUGENE FLORCZYK, *former class valedictorian and honor student, now vice-president of an advertising agency. Behind them is a large sign trimmed in green and brown that reads:* "WELCOME BACK: RYDELL HIGH, CLASS OF '59."

ALL

As I go trav'ling down life's highway
Whatever course my fortunes may foretell
I shall not go alone on my way
For thou shalt always be with me, Rydell.

When I seek rest from worldly matters
In palace or in hovel I may dwell
And though my bed be silk or tatters
My dreams shall always be of thee, Rydell.

EUGENE, PATTY *and* MISS LYNCH *enter.*

Through all the years, Rydell,
And tears, Rydell,
We give three cheers, Rydell, for thee.
Through ev'rything, Rydell,
We cling, Rydell,
And sing, Rydell, to thee.

As the song ends, MISS LYNCH *introduces* EUGENE *and then takes her seat.*

MISS LYNCH   Thank you. It is my pleasure at this time to introduce Mrs. Patricia Simcox Honeywell, your class yearbook editor, and Mr. Eugene Florczyk, class valedictorian and today vice-president of "Straight-Shooters Unlimited," Research and Marketing.

EUGENE   Miss Lynch, fellow graduates, honored guests, and others. Looking over these familiar faces really takes me back to those wonderful bygone days. Days of working and playing together, days of cheering together for our athletic teams—Yay, Ringtails! —and days of worrying together when examination time rolled around. Perhaps some of those familiar faces of yesteryear are absent this evening because they thought our beloved Miss Lynch might have one of her famous English finals awaiting us. *(To* MISS LYNCH*)* I was only joking. *(To audience)* However, the small portion of alumni I notice missing tonight are certainly not missing from our fond memories of them . . . and I'm sure they'd want us to know that they're fully present and accounted for in spirit, just the way we always remember them.

School bell rings—Chuck Berry-style guitar run is heard. The GREASERS *are revealed in positions of laziness, defiance, boredom and amusement.* THEY *sing a parody of the Alma Mater as* THEY *take over the stage.*

GREASERS

> I saw a dead skunk on the highway
> And I was goin' crazy from the smell
> 'Cause when the wind was blowin' my way
> It smelled just like the halls of old Rydell.
> And if ya gotta use the toilet
> And later on you start to scratch like hell,
> Take off your underwear and boil it
> 'Cause you got memories of old Rydell.

I can't explain, Rydell, this pain, Rydell.
Is it ptomaine Rydell gave me?
Is it v.d., Rydell? Could be, Rydell.
You oughta see the faculty.
If Mr. Clean, Rydell, had seen Rydell
He'd just turn green and disappear.
I'm outta luck, Rydell, dead duck, Rydell.
I'm stuck, Rydell, right here!

SCENE 2

The GREASERS *stalk off as the scene shifts to the high school cafeteria.* JAN *and* MARTY *enter, wearing their Pink Ladies jackets and carrying trays,* JAN's *loaded with food. As each female character enters, she joins the others at one large table.*

JAN   Jeez, I wish it was still summer. Christ, it's only a quarter after twelve and I feel like I been here a whole year already.

MARTY   Yeah, what a drag. Hey, you wanna sit here?

JAN   Yeah. Rizzo's comin', and Frenchy's bringin' that new chick. Hey, Marty, who'd ya get for Economics? Old Man Drucker?

MARTY   Yeah, what a pain in the ass. He keeps makin' passes.

JAN   For real? He never tried nothin' with me!

MARTY   Huh. You want my coleslaw?

JAN   I'll see if I have room for it. (SHE *takes coleslaw)*

MARTY   Hey, Rizzo, over here!

RIZZO *(Enters, carrying tray)* Hey, hey, hey! Hey, where's all the guys?

JAN Those slobs? You think they'd spend a dime on their lunch? They're baggin' it.

RIZZO Pretty cheap.

Lights fade on the cafeteria, come up on ROGER *and* DOODY *sitting on the school steps.*

DOODY Hey, Rump, I'll trade ya a sardine for a liver sausage.

ROGER I ain't eatin' one of those things. You had 'em in your icebox since last Easter.

DOODY Nah, this was a fresh can. My ma just opened it this morning.

ROGER You mean your old lady dragged her ass out of bed for ya?

DOODY Sure. She does it every year on the first day of school.

KENICKIE *(Enters)* Hey, where ya at?

ROGER Hey, Kenickie. What's happening?

DOODY Hey, Kenickie, whatcha got in the bag? I'll trade ya half a sardine.

KENICKIE Get outta here with that dog food. I ain't messin' up my stomach with none of that crap. *(HE pulls a pack of Hostess Sno-Balls out of the bag and starts unwrapping it)*

ROGER Hey, Kenicks, where were ya all summer?

KENICKIE What are you, the F.B.I.?

ROGER I was just askin'.

KENICKIE I was workin'. Which is more than either of you two skids can say.

ROGER Workin'! Yeah? Where?

KENICKIE Luggin' boxes at Bargain City.

ROGER Nice job!

KENICKIE Hey, eat me! I'm savin' up to get me some wheels. That's the only reason I took the job.

ROGER You gettin' a car, Kenick?

DOODY Hey, cool! What kind?

KENICKIE I don't know what kind yet, moron. But I got a name all picked out. "Greased Lightning!"

ROGER *(Putting him on)* Oh, nifty!

DOODY Yeah. Maybe you oughtta get a hamster instead.

DOODY *and* ROGER *laugh.*

KENICKIE Go ahead, laugh it up. When I show up in that baby, you suckers'll be laughin' out your ass.

ROGER Will we ever!

SONNY *enters wearing wraparound sunglasses. As* HE *enters,* HE *pulls a class schedule out of his pocket.*

KENICKIE   Hey, whattaya say, Sonny?

SONNY   Son of a bitch. I got old lady Lynch for English again. She hates my guts. *(Lights a cigarette)*

ROGER   Nah, she's got the hots for ya, Sonny. That's why she keeps puttin' ya back in her class.

KENICKIE   Yeah, she's just waitin' for ya to grow up.

SONNY   Yeah, well, this year she's gonna wish she never seen me.

KENICKIE   Yeah? What are ya gonna do to her?

SONNY   I'm just not gonna take any of her crap, that's all. I don't take no crap from nobody.

MISS LYNCH   *(Enters)* What's all the racket out here?

DOODY   Hi, Miss Lynch, did you have a nice summer?

SONNY   (HE *hides his cigarette by cupping it in his hand and shoving his hand in his pocket)* Hello, Miss Lynch, we was . . . uh . . .

MISS LYNCH   Dominic, aren't you supposed to be in class right now?

SONNY   I . . . I . . .

MISS LYNCH   You're just dawdling, aren't you? That's a fine way to start the new semester, Mr. LaTierri. Well? Are you going to stand there all day?

SONNY   No, ma'am

DOODY   No, ma'am.

MISS LYNCH Then move! *(Exits)*

SONNY Yes, Ma'am. *(HE takes his hand out of his pocket and inhales on the still-burning cigarette)*

ROGER I'm sure glad she didn't give you no crap, Son. You would have really told her off, right?

SONNY Shaddup.

Lights fade on steps, come up again on GIRLS in the cafeteria.

MARTY *(Squinting and putting her glasses on)* Hey, Jan, who's that chick with Frenchy? Is she the one you were tellin' me about?

JAN Yeah, her name's Sandy. She seems pretty cool. Maybe we could let her in the Pink Ladies.

RIZZO Just what we need. Another broad around.

FRENCHY *and* SANDY *enter, carrying trays.*

FRENCHY Hi, you guys, this is my new nextdoor neighbor, Sandy Dumbrowski. This here's Rizzo and that's Marty and you remember Jan.

JAN Sure. Hi.

SANDY Hi. Pleased to meet you.

FRENCHY *(To SANDY)* Come on, sit down. Hey, Marty, those new glasses?

MARTY Yeah, I just got 'em for school. Do they make me look smarter?

RIZZO   Nah. We can still see your face.

MARTY   How'dja like rice pudding down your bra?

JAN   *I'll* take it! *(SHE reaches over and grabs the pudding)*

RIZZO   How long you been livin' around here?

SANDY   Since July. My father just got transferred here.

MARTY   Hey, French, what'dja do to your hair? It really looks tough.

FRENCHY   Ah, I just touched it up a little.

JAN   You gonna eat your coleslaw, Sandy?

SANDY   It smells kinda funny.

FRENCHY   *(To divert SANDY's attention while JAN grabs her coleslaw)* Wait'll you have the chipped beef. Better known as "Shit on a Shingle."

MARTY   Don't mind her, Sandy. *Some* of us like to show off and use dirty words.

RIZZO   *Some* of us? Check out Miss Toilet-Mouth over here.

MARTY   *(Giving her "the finger")* Fuck you, Rizzle!

JAN   *(Trying to change the subject)* How do ya like the school so far, Sandy?

SANDY   Oh, it seems real nice. I was going to go to Immaculata, but my father had a fight with the Mother Superior over my patent leather shoes.

JAN   What do ya mean?

SANDY   She said boys could see up my dress in the reflection.

MARTY   Swear to God?

JAN   Hey, where do ya get shoes like that?

PATTY   *(Offstage)* Hi kids!

RIZZO   Hey, look who's comin'. Patty Simcox, the Little Lulu of Edgebrook Heights.

MARTY   Yeah. Wonder what she's doin' back here with us slobs?

RIZZO   Maybe she's havin' her period and wants to be alone.

PATTY   *(Enters)* Well, don't say hello.

RIZZO   We won't.

PATTY   Is there room at your table?

MARTY   *(Surprised)* Oh, yeah, move over, French.

PATTY   Oh, I just love the first day of school, don't you?

RIZZO   It's the biggest thrill of my life.

FRENCHY *starts doing* RIZZO's *hair.*

PATTY   You'll never guess what happened this morning.

RIZZO   Prob'ly not.

PATTY   Well, they announced this year's nominees for the Student Council, and guess who's up for vice-president?

MARTY   *(Knowing what's coming)* Who?

PATTY   Me! Isn't that wild?

RIZZO   Wild.

PATTY   I just hope I don't make *too* poor a showing.

RIZZO   Well, we sure wish ya all the luck in the world.

PATTY   Oh, uh, thanks. Oh, you must think I'm a terrible clod! I never even bothered to introduce myself to your new friend.

SANDY   Oh, I'm Sandy Dumbrowski.

PATTY   It's a real pleasure, Sandy. We certainly are glad to have you here at Rydell.

SANDY   Thank you.

PATTY   I'll bet you're going to be at the cheerleader tryouts next week, aren't you?

SANDY   Oh, no. I'd be too embarrassed.

PATTY   Don't be silly. I could give you a few pointers if you like.

MARTY   Aaaaahhh, son of a bitch!

PATTY   Goodness gracious!

RIZZO   Nice language. What was that all about?

MARTY   *(Examining her glasses)* One of my diamonds fell in the macaroni.

Lights fade on GIRLS, *come up on* GUYS *on the steps.*

DOODY   Hey, ain't that Danny over there?

SONNY   Where?

KENICKIE   Yeah. What's he doin' hangin' around the girls' gym entrance?

ROGER   Maybe he's hot for some chick!

SONNY   One of those skanks we've seen around since kindergarten? Not quite.

DOODY   *(Yells) Hey, Danny! Whatcha doin'?*

ROGER   That's good, Dood. Play it real cool.

KENICKIE   Aw, leave him alone. Maybe he ain't gettin' any.

DANNY   *(Enters, carrying books and lunch)* Hey, you guys, how they hangin'? *(Fakes* SONNY *out with a quick goose)*

SONNY   Whattaya say, Zuko—'dja see any good-lookin' meat over there?

DANNY   Nah, just the same old chicks everybody's made it with!

DOODY   Where ya been all summer, Danny?

DANNY   Well, I spent a lot of time down at the beach.

KENICKIE   Hey, 'dja meet any new broads?

DANNY   Nah. Just met this one who was sorta cool, ya know?

SONNY   Ya mean she "puts out?"

DANNY   Is that all you ever think about, Sonny?

SONNY   *(Looking around at the other* GUYS*)* Fuckin' A!

ROGER   Aahh, come off it, Zuko. Ya got in her drawers, right?

DANNY   Look, man. That's none of you guys' business.

KENICKIE   Okay, if that's the way you're gonna be.

DANNY   You don't want to hear all the horny details, anyway.

SONNY   *(Starts tickling* DANNY*)* Sure we do! Let's hear a little!

ROGER   *(Joining in)* C'mon, Zuko, koochee koochee!

> ALL GUYS *join in playfully mauling* DANNY *as the lights fade on them and come back up on the* GIRLS *at the cafeteria table.*

SANDY   I spent most of the summer at the beach.

JAN   What for? We got a brand new pool right in the neighborhood. It's real nice.

RIZZO   Yeah, if ya like swimmin' in Clorox.

SANDY   Well—actually, I met a boy there.

MARTY   You hauled your ass all the way to the beach for some guy?

SANDY   This was sort of a special boy.

RIZZO   Are you kiddin'? There ain't no such thing.

Lights stay up on GIRLS, *come up on* GUYS.

DANNY Okay, you guys, ya wanna know what happened?

GUYS Yeah! Let's hear it! *Etc. ad lib.*

SANDY No, he was really nice. It was all very romantic.

> DANNY *rises and sings "Summer Nights" to the* GUYS. SANDY *sings her version to the* GIRLS.

DANNY	Summer lovin'! Had me a blast.
SANDY	Summer lovin'! Happened so fast.
DANNY	Met a girl crazy for me.
SANDY	Met a boy cute as can be.

BOTH

Summer day, drifting away, to
Uh-oh, those summer nights.

GUYS	Tell me more, tell me more,
	Didja get very far?
GIRLS	Tell me more, tell me more,
MARTY	Like does he have a car?
DANNY	She swam by me, she got a cramp.
SANDY	He ran by me, got my suit damp.
DANNY	Saved her life, she nearly drowned.
SANDY	He showed off, splashing around.

BOTH

Summer sun, something begun, then
Uh-oh, those summer nights.

GIRLS	Tell me more, tell me more.
FRENCH.	Was it love at first sight?

GUYS   Tell me more, tell me more.
KENICK.   Did she put up a fight?
DANNY   Took her bowling, in the arcade.
SANDY   We went strolling, drank lemonade.
DANNY   We made out, under the dock.
SANDY   We stayed out till ten o'clock.

BOTH

Summer fling, don't mean a thing, but
Uh-oh, those summer nights.

GUYS   Tell me more, tell me more,
         But ya don't have to brag.
GIRLS   Tell me more, tell me more.
RIZZO   'Cause he sounds like a drag.
SANDY   He got friendly, holding my hand.
DANNY   She got friendly, down on the sand.
SANDY   He was sweet, just turned eighteen.
DANNY   She was good, ya know what I mean?

BOTH

Summer heat, boy and girl meet, then
Uh-oh, those summer nights!

GIRLS   Tell me more, tell me more,
JAN   How much dough did he spend?
GUYS   Tell me more, tell me more,
SONNY   Could she get me a friend?
SANDY   It turned colder, that's where it ends.
DANNY   So I told her we'd still be friends.
SANDY   Then we made our true love vow.
DANNY   Wonder what she's doin' now.

BOTH

Summer dreams, ripped at the seams, but
Uh-ohh! Those summer nights!

Lights stay up on both groups after song.

PATTY   Gee, he sounds wonderful, Sandy.

DOODY   She really sounds cool, Danny.

RIZZO   A guy doesn't touch ya and it's true love. Maybe he was a fairy.

SANDY *gives* RIZZO *a puzzled look.*

ROGER   Big knockers, huh?

FRENCHY   Hey, nice talk, Rizzo!

KENICKIE   She Catholic?

JAN   What if we said that about Danny Zuko?

SONNY   Hot box, huh, Zuker?

SANDY   Did you say Danny Zuko?

DANNY   I didn't say that, Sonny!

RIZZO   Hey, was he the guy?

DOODY   Boy, you get all the neats!

SANDY   Doesn't he go to Lake Forest Academy?

PINK LADIES *laugh.*

KENICKIE   She doesn't go to Rydell, does she?

DANNY *shakes his head "no."*

MARTY   That's a laugh!

SONNY   Too bad, I'd bet she'd go for me.

PATTY   *(Confidentially)* Listen, Sandy, forget Danny Zuko. I know some really sharp boys.

RIZZO   So do I. Right, you guys? C'mon, let's go.

PINK LADIES *get up from the table,* SANDY *following them. The* GUYS *all laugh together.*

FRENCHY   See ya 'round, Patty!

RIZZO   Yeah, maybe we'll drop in on the next Student Council meeting.

RIZZO *nudges* MARTY *in the ribs. Lights go down on the lunch-room.* GIRLS *cross toward* GUYS *on steps.*

MARTY   Well, speaking of the devil!

SONNY   *(To* GUYS*)* What'd I tell ya, they're always chasin' me.

MARTY   *(Pushing* SONNY *away)* Not you, greaseball! Danny!

RIZZO   Yeah. We got a surprise for ya.

PINK LADIES *shove* SANDY *toward* DANNY.

SANDY   *(Surprised and nervous)* Hello, Danny.

DANNY   *(Uptight)* Oh, hi. How are ya?

SANDY   Fine.

DANNY   Oh yeah . . . I . . . uh . . . thought you were goin' to Immaculata.

SANDY   I changed my plans.

DANNY   Yeah! Well, that's cool. I'll see ya around. Let's go, you guys. *(Pushes* GUYS *out)*

DOODY   Where do you know her from, Danny?

DANNY   Huh? Oh, just an old friend of my family's.

SONNY   *(To* DANNY*)* She's pretty sharp. I think she's got eyes for me, didja notice?

> DANNY *gives* SONNY *"a look," pulls him off.* GUYS *exit.*

JAN   *(Picking up* DANNY*'s lunch)* Gee, he was so glad to see ya, he dropped his lunch.

SANDY   I don't get it. He was so nice this summer.

FRENCHY   Don't worry about it, Sandy.

MARTY   Hey listen, how'd you like to come over to my house tonight? It'll be just us girls.

JAN   Yeah, those guys are all a bunch of creeps.

> DANNY *returns for his lunch.*

RIZZO   Yeah, Zuko's the biggest creep of all.

> RIZZO, *seeing* DANNY, *exits. Other* GIRLS *follow.*

SCENE 3

School bell rings and class change begins. GREASERS, PATTY *and* EUGENE *enter, go to lockers, get books, etc.* DANNY *sees* DOODY *with guitar.*

DANNY   Hey, Doody, where'dja get the guitar?

DOODY   I just started takin' lessons this summer.

DANNY   Can you play anything on it?

DOODY   Sure. *(HE fumbles with the frets and strikes a sour chord)* That's a C. *(HE sits and waits for approval)*

MARTY   *(Baffled)* Hey, that's pretty good.

DOODY   *(Hitting each chord)* Then I know an A minor, and an F, and I've been workin' on a G.

FRENCHY   Hey! Can you play "Tell Laura I Love Her?"

DOODY   I don't know. Has it got a C in it?

DANNY   Hey, come on; let's hear a little, Elvis.

DOODY   *(Pulling out instruction book)* "Magic Changes," by Ronnie Dell . . . *(Sings off key while strumming sour chords)*

    C-C-C-C-C-C
    A-A-A-A minor
    F-F-F-F-F-F
    G-G-G-G seventh

DANNY   That's terrific.

DOODY   Thanks—want to hear it again?

ALL   Sure! Yeah! *(Etc. ad lib)*

    DOODY *starts to sing "Those Magic Changes," and other* KIDS *transform into rock 'n roll, "doo-wop" group backing him as* HE *suddenly becomes a teen idol rock 'n roll star.*

DOODY and GROUP

C-C-C-C-C-C
A-A-A-A minor
F-F-F-F-F-F
G-G-G-G seventh

What's that playing on the radio?
Why do I start swaying to and fro?
I have never heard that song before
But if I don't hear it any more
It's still familiar to me,
Sends a thrill right through me,
'Cause those chords remind me of
The night that I first fell in love to
Those magic changes.

My heart arranges
a melody
That's never the same.
A melody
That's calling your name
And begs you, please, come back to me,
Please return to me,
Don't go away again.
Oh, make them play again
The music I long to hear
As once again you whisper in my ear.
Ohhhh, my darling.

I'll be waiting by the radio.
You'll come back to me someday, I know.
Been so lonesome since your last goodbye
But I'm singing as I cry-y-y.
While the bass is sounding,
While the drums are pounding,
Beating of my broken heart
Will climb to first place on the chart.
Ohhh, my heart arranges
Ohhh, those magic changes.

C-C-C-C-C-C
A-A-A-A minor
F-F-F-F-F-F
G-G-G-G seventh
Shoop-doo-wah bom!

At the end of the song, MISS LYNCH *enters to break up the group.*
ALL *exit except* GUYS *and* SONNY.

MISS LYNCH *(To* SONNY*)* Mr. LaTierri, aren't you due in Detention
Hall right now?

GUYS *all make fun of* SONNY *and lead him off to Detention Hall.*

SCENE 4

A pajama party in MARTY*'s bedroom.* MARTY, FRENCHY, JAN *and*
RIZZO *are in pastel baby-doll pajamas,* SANDY *in a quilted robe
buttoned all the way up to the neck. The WAXX jingle for the
Vince Fontaine Show is playing on the radio.*

VINCE'S VOICE Hey, hey, this is the Main Brain, Vince Fontaine, at
Big Fifteen! Spinnin' the stacks of wax, here at the House of
Wax—W-A-X-X. *(OOO-ga horn sound)* Cruisin' time, 10:46.
(Sound of ricocheting bullet) Sharpshooter pick hit of the week.
A brand new one shootin' up the charts like a rocket by The
Vel-doo Rays—goin' out to Ronnie and Sheila, the kids down
at Mom's School Store, and especially to Little Joe and the
LaDons—listen in while I give it a spin! *(Radio fades).*

FRENCHY *(Looking at a fan magazine that has a big picture of Fabian
on the cover)* Hey, it says here that Fabian is in love with some
Swedish movie star and might be gettin' married.

JAN Oh, no!

MARTY   Who cares, as long as they don't get their hooks into Kookie.

RIZZO   Hey, Frenchy, throw me a ciggie-butt, will ya?

FRENCHY *throws* RIZZO *a cigarette.*

MARTY   Me too, while ya got the pack out.

FRENCHY   Ya want one, Sandy?

SANDY   Oh, no thanks. I don't smoke.

FRENCHY   Ya don't? Didja ever try it?

SANDY   Well, no, but . . .

RIZZO   Go on, try it. It ain't gonna kill ya. Give her a Hit Parade!

FRENCHY *throws* SANDY *a Hit Parade.*

Now, when she holds up the match, suck in on it.

FRENCHY *lights the cigarette,* SANDY *inhales and starts coughing violently.*

Oh, I shoulda told ya, don't inhale if you're not used to it.

MARTY   That's okay. You'll get better at it.

FRENCHY   Yeah, then I'll show ya how to French inhale. That's really cool. Watch. (SHE *demonstrates French inhaling)*

JAN   Phtyyaaagghh! That's the ugliest thing I ever saw!

FRENCHY   Nah, the guys really go for it. That's how I got my nickname, Frenchy.

RIZZO   Sure it is. Jesus Christ, you guys, I almost forgot! *(SHE removes a half-gallon of wine from her overnight bag)* A little Sneaky Pete to get the party goin'.

JAN   Italian Swiss Colony. Wow, it's imported.

RIZZO *passes bottle to* MARTY.

FRENCHY   Hey, we need some glasses.

RIZZO   Just drink it out of the bottle, we ain't got cooties.

MARTY   It's kind of sweet. I think I like Thunderbird better.

RIZZO   Okay, Princess Grace. *(Takes bottle away from* MARTY*)*

MARTY   *(Grabbing bottle back)* I didn't say I didn't want any, it just don't taste very strong, that's all.

MARTY *passes bottle to* SANDY, *who quickly passes it to* JAN.

JAN   Hey, I brought some Twinkies, anybody want one?

MARTY   Twinkies and wine? That's real class, Jan.

JAN   *(Pointing to label on bottle)* It says right here it's a dessert wine! *(Passes wine to* FRENCHY*)*

RIZZO   Hey, Sandy didn't get any wine. *(Hands bottle to* SANDY*)*

SANDY   Oh, that's okay. I don't mind.

RIZZO   Hey, I'll bet you never had a drink before either.

SANDY   Sure I did. I had some champagne at my cousin's wedding once.

RIZZO   Oh, ring-a-ding-ding. *(Hands her wine)*

SANDY *sips wine cautiously.*

Hey, no! Ya gotta chug it. Like this! *(RIZZO takes a big slug from the bottle)* Otherwise you swallow air bubbles and that's what makes you throw up.

JAN   I never knew that.

MARTY   Sure, Rudy from the Capri Lounge told me the same thing.

SANDY *takes a slug from the bottle and holds it in her mouth, trying to swallow it.*

JAN   Hey, Sandy, you ever wear earrings? I think they'd keep your face from lookin' so skinny.

MARTY   Hey! Yeah! I got some big round ones made out of real mink. They'd look great on you.

FRENCHY   Wouldja like me to pierce your ears for ya, Sandy? I'm gonna be a beautician, y'know.

JAN   Yeah, she's real good. She did mine for me.

SANDY   Oh no, my father'd probably kill me.

MARTY   You still worry about what your old man thinks?

SANDY   Well . . . no. But isn't it awfully dangerous?

RIZZO   *(Leans down to SANDY)* You ain't afraid, are ya?

SANDY   Of course not!

FRENCHY   Good. Hey, Marty, you got a needle around? *(SHE rummages in dresser for needle)*

MARTY   Hey, how about my virgin pin! *(SHE reaches for her Pink*

Ladies jacket and takes off "circle pin," handing it to FRENCHY)

JAN   Nice to know it's good for somethin'.

MARTY   What's that crack supposed to mean?

JAN   Forget it, Marty, I was just teasing ya.

MARTY   Yeah, well, tease somebody else. It's my house.

FRENCHY *begins to pierce* SANDY*'s ears.* SANDY *yelps.*

FRENCHY   Hey, would ya hold still!

MARTY   *(To the rescue)* Hey, French . . . why don't you take Sandy in the john? My old lady'd kill me if we got blood all over the rug.

SANDY   Huh?

FRENCHY   It only bleeds for a second. Come on.

JAN   Aaaww! We miss all the fun!

JAN *opens a second package of Twinkies as* FRENCHY *begins to lead* SANDY *off.*

FRENCHY   Hey, Marty, I need some ice to numb her earlobes.

MARTY   *(Exasperated)* Ahh . . . look, why don'tcha just let the cold water run for a little while, then stick her ear under the faucet?

SANDY   Listen, I'm sorry, but I'm not feeling too well, and I . . .

RIZZO   Look, Sandy, if you think you're gonna be hangin' around with the Pink Ladies—you gotta get with it! Otherwise, forget it . . . and go back to your hot cocoa and Girl Scout cookies!

SANDY   Okay, come on . . . Frenchy.

JAN   Hey, Sandy, don't sweat it. If she screws up, she can always fix your hair so your ears won't show.

FRENCHY   Smart ass.

RIZZO   That chick's gettin' to be a real pain in the ass.

JAN   Ah, lay off, Rizzo.

MARTY   Yeah, she can't help it if she ain't been around.

RIZZO   Yeah, well, how long are we supposed to play babysitter for her?

Suddenly a loud "urp" sound is heard offstage.

What the hell was that?

The GIRLS *all look at each other, bewildered, for a couple of seconds, then* FRENCHY *runs back into the room.*

FRENCHY   Hey, Marty, Sandy's sick. She's heavin' all over the place!

JAN   Dja do her ears already?

FRENCHY   Nah. I only did one. As soon as she saw the blood she went *bleugh!*

RIZZO   God! What a party poop!

MARTY   Jeez, it's gettin' kinda chilly. I think I'll put my robe on. (SHE *pulls out a gaudy kimono and makes a big show of putting it on)*

JAN   Hey, Marty, where'dja get that thing?

MARTY   Oh, you like it? It's from Japan.

RIZZO   Yeah, everything's made in Japan these days.

MARTY   No, this guy I know sent it to me.

FRENCHY   No kiddin'!

JAN   You goin' with a Jap?

MARTY   He ain't a Jap, stupid. He's a Marine. And a real doll, too.

FRENCHY   Oh, wow! Hey, Marty, can he get me one of those things?

JAN   You never told us you knew any Marines.

RIZZO   How long you known this guy?

MARTY   Oh . . . just a couple of months. I met him on a blind date at the roller rink . . . and the next thing I know, he joins up. Anyway, right off the bat he starts sendin' me things—and then today I got this kimono. *(Trying to be cool)* Oh yeah, look what else! (SHE *takes a ring out of her cleavage)*

FRENCHY   Oh, neat!

MARTY   It's just a tiny bit too big. So I gotta get some angora for it.

FRENCHY   Jeez! Engaged to a Marine!

RIZZO   *(Sarcastically)* Endsville.

JAN   What's this guy look like, Marty?

FRENCHY   You got a picture?

MARTY   Yeah, but it's not too good. He ain't in uniform. (SHE *takes*

*her wallet out of the dresser. It's one of those fat bulging ones
with rubber bands around it.* SHE *swings wallet and accordion
picture folder drops to floor)* Oh, here it is . . . next to Paul Anka.

JAN How come it's ripped in half?

MARTY Oh, his old girlfriend was in the picture.

JAN What's this guy's name, anyway?

MARTY Oh! It's Freddy. Freddy Strulka.

JAN He a Polack?

MARTY Naah, I think he's Irish.

FRENCHY Do you write him a lot, Marty?

MARTY Pretty much. Every time I get a present.

JAN Whattaya say to a guy in a letter, anyway?

MARTY *and* GIRLS *suddenly become a rock 'n roll quartet and sing
"Freddy, My Love."*

MARTY

Freddy, my love, I miss you more than words can say.
Freddy, my love, please keep in touch while you're away.
Hearing from you can make the day so much better,
Getting a souvenir or maybe a letter.
I really flipped over the gray cashmere sweater.
Freddy, my love
(Freddy, my love, Freddy, my love, Freddy, my lo-oove.)

Freddy, you know, your absence makes me feel so blue.
That's okay, though, your presents make me think of you.
My ma will have a heart attack when she catches

Those pedal pushers with the black leather patches.
Oh, how I wish I had a jacket that matches.
Freddy, my love
(Freddy, my love, Freddy, my love, Freddy, my lo-oove)

Don't keep your letters from me,
I thrill to every line.
Your spelling's kinda crummy
But honey, so is mine.
I treasure every giftie,
The ring is really nifty.
You say it cost you fifty
So you're thrifty,
I don't mind!
(Woe-ohh-ohh-oh)

Freddy, you'll see, you'll hold me in your arms someday
And I will be wearing your lacy lonjeray.
Thinking about it, my heart's pounding already
Knowing when you come home we're bound to go steady
And throw your service pay around like confetti
Freddy, my love
(Freddy, my love, Freddy, my love, Freddy, my lo-oove)

On the last few bars of song the GIRLS *fall asleep one by one, until* RIZZO *is the only one left awake.* SHE *pulls pants on over her pajamas and climbs out the window. Just at that moment,* SANDY *comes back into the room, unnoticed by* RIZZO, *and stands looking after her.*

SCENE 5

GUYS *come running on, out of breath and carrying quarts of beer and four hubcaps.* DANNY *has a tire iron.*

DANNY   I don't know why I brought this tire iron! I coulda yanked these babies off with my bare hands!

SONNY Sure ya could, Zuko! I just broke six fingernails!

ROGER Hey, you guys, these hubcaps ain't got a scratch on 'em. They must be worth two beans apiece easy.

DOODY No kiddin'? Hey, how much can we get for these dice? *(Pulls out foam rubber dice)*

ROGER Hey, who the hell would put brand new chromers on a second-hand dodgem car!

DANNY Probably some real tool!

SONNY Hey, c'mon, let's go push these things off on somebody!

DANNY Eleven o'clock at night? Sure, maybe we could go sell 'em at a police station!

DOODY A police station, what a laugh! They don't use these kinda hubcaps on cop cars.

A car horn is heard.

SONNY Hey, here comes that car we just hit! Let's tear ass! Ditch the evidence!

GUYS run, dropping hubcaps. SONNY tries to scoop them up as KENICKIE drives on in "Greased Lightning."

DANNY Hey, wait a minute—it's Kenickie!

KENICKIE All right, put those things back on the car, dipshit!

SONNY Jeez, whatta grouch! We was only holdin' 'em for ya so nobody'd swipe 'em.

DOODY *(Handing back dice)* Hey, where'dja get these cool dice?

DANNY   Kenickie, whattaya doin' with this hunka junk, anyway?

KENICKIE   Whattaya mean? This is "Greased Lightning!"

"Whats" and puzzled looks go up from the GUYS.

SONNY   What? You really expect to cop some snatch in this sardine can?

KENICKIE   Hey, get bent, LaTierri!

ROGER   Nice color, what is it? Candy-Apple Primer?

KENICKIE   That's all right—wait till I give it a paint job and soup up the engine—she'll work like a champ!

DANNY   *(Looking at car and picking up mike)* The one and only Greased Lightning!

Hard-driving guitar begins playing "Greased Lightnin'."

KENICKIE

> I'll have me overhead lifters and four-barrel quads, oh, yeah.
> A fuel-injection cutoff and chrome-plated rods, oh, yeah.
> With a four-speed on the floor, they'll be waitin' at the door.
> Ya know that ain't no shit, I'll be gettin' lotsa tit
> In Greased Lightnin'.

KENICKIE and GUYS

> Go, Greased Lightnin', you're burnin' up the quarter mile.
> (Greased Lightnin', go, Greased Lightnin')
> Yeah, Greased Lightnin', you're coastin' through the heat-lap trials.
> (Greased Lightnin', yeah, Greased Lightnin')
> You are supreme
> The chicks'll cream
> For Greased Lightnin'!

KENICKIE

> I'll have me purple frenched tail-lights and thirty-inch fins, oh,
> yeah.
> A palomino dashboard and dual-muffler twins, oh, yeah.
> With new pistons, plugs, and shocks, I can get off my rocks.
> Ya know that I ain't braggin', she's a real pussy-wagon.
> Greased Lightnin'!

KENICKIE and GUYS

> Go, Greased Lightnin', you're burnin' up the quarter mile.
> (Greased Lightnin', go, Greased Lightnin')
> Yeah, Greased Lightnin', you're coastin' through the heat-lap
> trials.
> (Greased. Lightnin', yeah, Greased Lightnin')
> You are supreme
> The chicks'll cream
> For Greased Lightnin'!

> *As song ends,* RIZZO *enters.*

RIZZO What the hell is that thing?

KENICKIE Hey, what took you so long?

RIZZO Never mind what took me so long. Is that your new custom
convert?

KENICKIE This is it! Ain't it cool?

RIZZO Yeah, it's about as cool as a Good Humor truck.

KENICKIE Okay, Rizzo, if that's how you feel, why don'tcha go back
to the pajama party? Plenty of chicks would give their right tit
to ride around in this little number.

RIZZO Sure they would! Out! What do ya think this is, a gangbang?
*(*SHE *opens the passenger door, shoving* GUYS *out)* Hey, Danny!

I just left your girl friend at Marty's house, flashin' all over the place.

DANNY Whattaya talkin' about?

RIZZO Sandy Dumbrowski! Y'know . . . Sandra Dee.

KENICKIE Be cool, you guys.

RIZZO *immediately starts crawling all over him.*

DANNY Hey, you better tell that to Rizzo!

Siren sounds.

KENICKIE The fuzz! Hey, you guys better get ridda those hub-caps.

DANNY Whattaya mean, man? They're yours!

KENICKIE Oh no they're not. I stole 'em. (HE *starts to drive off)*

Siren sounds again. GUYS *leap on car and drive off, singing, "Greased Lightning" as the lights change.*

SCENE 6

SANDY *runs on with pom-poms, dressed in a green baggy gymsuit.* SHE *does a Rydell cheer.*

SANDY

Do a split, give a yell,
Throw a fit for old Rydell.
Way to go, green and brown,
Turn the foe upside down.

SANDY *does awkward split.* DANNY *enters.*

DANNY   Hiya, Sandy.

SANDY *gives him a look and turns her head so that* DANNY *sees the Band-Aid on her ear.*

Hey, what happened to your ear?

SANDY   Huh? *(*SHE *covers her ear with her hand, answers coldly)* Oh, nothing. Just an accident.

DANNY   Hey, look, uh, I hope you're not bugged about that first day at school. I mean, couldn't ya tell I was glad to see ya?

SANDY   Well, you could've been a little nicer to me in front of your friends.

DANNY   Are you kidding? Hey, you don't know those guys. They just see ya talkin' to a chick and right away they think she puts . . . well, you know what I mean.

SANDY   I'm not sure. It looked to me like maybe you had a new girlfriend or something.

DANNY   Are you kiddin'! Listen, if it was up to me, I'd never even look at any other chick but you.

SANDY *blushes.*

Hey, tell ya what. We're throwin' a party in the park tonight for Frenchy. She's gonna quit school before she flunks again and go to Beauty School. Howdja like to make it on down there with me?

SANDY   I'd really like to, but I'm not so sure those girls want me around anymore.

DANNY   Listen, Sandy. Nobody's gonna start gettin' salty with ya when I'm around. Uh-uhh!

SANDY   All right, Danny, as long as you're with me. Let's not let anyone come between us again, okay?

PATTY   *(Rushing onstage with two batons and wearing cheerleader outfit)* Hiiiiiiiii, Danny! Oh, don't let me interrupt. *(Gives* SANDY *baton)* Here, Sandy, why don't you twirl this for a while. *(Taking* DANNY *aside)* I've been dying to tell you something. You know what I found out after you left my house the other night? My mother thinks you're cute. *(To* SANDY*)* He's such a lady-killer.

SANDY   Isn't he, though! *(Out of corner of mouth, to* DANNY*)* What were you doing at her house?

DANNY   Ah, I was just copying down some homework.

PATTY   Come on, Sandy, let's practice. *(Begins twirling baton)*

SANDY   Yeah, let's! I'm just dying to make a good impression on all those cute lettermen.

DANNY   Oh, that's why you're wearing that thing—gettin' ready to show off your skivvies to a bunch of horny jocks?

SANDY   Don't tell me you're jealous, Danny.

DANNY   What? Of that buncha meatheads! Don't make me laugh. Ha! Ha!

SANDY   Just because they can do something you can't do?

DANNY   Yeah, sure, right.

SANDY   Okay, what have *you* ever done?

DANNY *(To* PATTY, *twirling baton)* Stop that! *(Thinking a moment)* I won a Hully Gully contest at the "Teen Talent" record hop.

SANDY Aaahh, you don't even know what I'm talking about.

DANNY Whattaya mean, look, I could run circles around those jerks.

SANDY But you'd rather spend your time copying other people's homework.

DANNY Listen, the next time they have tryouts for any of those teams I'll show you what I can do.

PATTY Oh, what a lucky coincidence! The track team's having tryouts tomorrow.

DANNY *(Panic)* Huh? Okay, I'll be there.

SANDY Big talk.

DANNY You think so, huh? Hey, Patty, when'dja say those tryouts were?

PATTY Tomorrow, tenth period, on the football field.

DANNY Good, I'll be there. You're gonna come watch me, aren't you?

PATTY Oooohh, I can't wait!

DANNY Solid. I'll see ya there, sexy. *(Exits)*

PATTY Toodles! *(Elated, turns to* SANDY*)* Ooohh, I'm so excited, aren't you?

SANDY Come on, let's practice.

SANDY and PATTY *(Sing Rydell fight song, twirling batons, SANDY just missing PATTY's head with each swing)*

> Hit 'em again, Rydell Ringtails.
> Tear 'em apart, green and brown.
> Bash their brains out, stomp 'em on the floor
> For the glory of Rydell evermore.
>
> Fight, team, fight; fight, team, fight.
> Chew 'em up—spit 'em out.
> Fight, team, fight.

SANDY *and* PATTY *exit doing majorette march step.*

SCENE 7

A deserted section of the park. JAN *and* ROGER *on picnic table.* RIZZO *and* KENICKIE *making out on bench.* MARTY *sitting on other bench.* FRENCHY *and* SONNY *on blanket reading fan magazines.* DANNY *pacing.* DOODY *sitting on a trash can. They're all eating food or drinking beer. A portable radio is playing The Vince Fontaine Show.*

VINCE'S RADIO VOICE   Hey, gettin' back on the rebound here for our second half. *(Cuckoo sound)* Dancin' Word Bird Contest comin' up in a half hour, when maybe I'll call you. Hey, I think you'll like this little ditty from the city, a new group discovered by Alan Freed. Turn up the sound and stomp on the ground. Ohhh, yeah!!! *(Radio fades)*

DANNY   Hey, Frenchy, when do ya start beauty school?

FRENCHY   Next week. I can hardly wait. No more dumb books and stupid teachers.

MARTY   *(Holding out a package of Vogues)* Hey, anybody want a Vogue?

FRENCHY   Yeah, you got any pink ones left?

SONNY   Yeah, give me one. *(Puts it in his mouth)* How about one for later?

MARTY   *(Throwing him another cigarette)* God, what a mooch!

DOODY   Hey, Rump, you shouldn't be eatin' that cheeseburger. It's still Friday, y'know!

ROGER   Son-of-a-bitch! What'dja remind me for? Now I gotta go to confession. *(HE takes another bite of the cheeseburger)*

JAN   Well, I can eat anything. That's the nice thing about bein' a Lutheran.

ROGER   Yeah, that's the nice thing about bein' Petunia Pig.

JAN   *(Giving ROGER "the finger")* Hey, right here, lard-ass!

FRENCHY   Hey, Sonny, don't maul that magazine. There's a picture of Ricky Nelson in there I really wanna save.

SONNY   I was just lookin' at Shelley Farberay's jugs.

FRENCHY   *(Leaning over to look at picture and primping)* Y'know, lotsa people think I look just like Shelley Farberries.

SONNY   Not a chance. You ain't got a set like hers.

FRENCHY   I happen to know she wears falsies.

SONNY   You oughtta know, foam-domes.

JAN   You want another cheeseburger?

ROGER   Nah, I think I'll have a Coke.

JAN   You shouldn't drink so much Coke. It rots your teeth.

ROGER   No shit, Bucky Beaver.

JAN   I ain't kiddin'. Somebody told me about this scientist once who knocked out one of his teeth and dropped it in this glass of Coke, and after a week, the tooth rotted away until there was nothing left.

ROGER   For Christ's sake, I ain't gonna carry a mouthful of Coke around for a week. Besides, what do you care what I do with my teeth? It ain't your problem.

JAN   No, I guess not.

MARTY   *(Wearing extra-large college letterman sweater and modeling for DANNY)* Hey, Danny, how would I look as a college girl?

DANNY   *(Pinching boobs)* Boola-boola . . .

MARTY   Hey, watch it! It belongs to this big jock at Holy Contrition.

DANNY   *(Indicating MARTY 's sweater)* Wait'll ya see me wearin' one of those things. I'm gonna try out for the track team tomorrow.

SEVERAL HEADS *turn and look at* DANNY. *Ad libs of* "What?" "Zuko, no!," *etc.*

MARTY   Are you serious? With those bird legs?

KIDS *all laugh.* ROGER *does funny imitation of* DANNY *as a gung-ho track star.*

DANNY   Hey, better hobby than yours, Rump.

Other GUYS *laugh at remark,* ALL *giving* ROGER *calls of* "Rump-Rump."

JAN *(After a pause)* How come you never get mad at those guys?

ROGER Why should I?

JAN Well, that name they call you. Rump!

ROGER That's just my nickname. It's sorta like a title.

JAN Whattaya mean?

ROGER I'm king of the mooners.

JAN The what?

ROGER I'm the mooning champ of Rydell High.

JAN You mean showin' off your bare behind to people? That's pretty raunchy.

ROGER Nah, it's neat! I even mooned old Lady Lynch once. I hung one on her right out the car window. And she never even knew who it was.

JAN Too much! I wish I'd been there. *(Quickly)* I mean . . . y'know what I mean.

ROGER Yeah. I wish you'd been there, too.

JAN *(Seriously)* You do?

ROGER *(Answers her by singing "Mooning")*

> I spend my days just mooning,
> So sad and blue.
> I spend my nights just mooning
> All over you.

JAN All over who?

ROGER

> Oh, I'm so full of love,
> As any fool can see, ·
> 'Cause angels up above
> Have hung a moon on me.

JAN Why must you go?

ROGER

> Why must I go on mooning
> So all alone.
> There would be no more mooning
> If you would

JAN Call me up on the phone.

ROGER

> Oh, lying by myself in bed I
> Cry and give myself the red eye
> Mooning over you.
> I'll stand behind you mooning
> Forevermore.

JAN Forevermore.

ROGER

> Someday you'll find me mooning
> At your front door.

JAN At my front door!

ROGER

> Oh, every day at school I watch ya

Always will until I gotcha
Mooning, too.
(There's a moon out tonight!)

DOODY   *(Loudly)* Hey, Danny, there's that chick ya know.

SANDY *and* EUGENE *enter,* EUGENE *wearing Bermuda shorts and argyle socks.* BOTH *have bags of leaves.* RIZZO *and* KENICKIE *sit up to look.* DANNY *moves to* EUGENE *and stares.*

EUGENE   Well, Sandy, I think I have all the leaves I want. Uh . . . why don't I wait for you with Dad in the station wagon.

DANNY, *looking at* EUGENE, *outlines a square with head movement.* EUGENE *exits. As* DANNY *walks away,* SONNY *crosses to* SANDY.

SONNY   Hi ya, Sandy. What's shakin'? How 'bout a beer?

SANDY   *(Giving* DANNY *a look)* No, thanks, I can't stay.

DANNY   Oh, yeah! Then whattaya doin' hangin' around? *(HE casually puts his hand on* MARTY*'s shoulder and* MARTY *looks at him, bewildered)*

SANDY   I just came out to collect some leaves for Biology.

SONNY   Oh, yeah? There's some really neat yellow ones over by the drainage canal. C'mon, I'll show ya'! *(HE grabs* SANDY *and starts off)*

KENICKIE   *(Shouting)* Those ain't leaves. They're used rubbers.

SONNY *gives* KENICKIE *a look as* HE *drags* SANDY *offstage.*

DOODY   Hey, Danny . . . aren't you gonna follow 'em?

DANNY   Why should I? She don't mean nothin' to me.

RIZZO *(To* DANNY*)* Sure, Zuko, every day now! Ya mean you ain't told 'em?

KENICKIE Told us what?

RIZZO Oh, nothin'. Right, Zuko?

KENICKIE Come off it, Rizzo. Whattaya tryin' to do, make us think she's like you?

RIZZO What's that crack supposed to mean? I ain't heard you complainin'.

KENICKIE That's 'cause ya been sittin' on my face all night.

DANNY Hey, cool it, huh?

RIZZO Yeah, Kenickie, if you don't shut up it's gonna be your ass.

KENICKIE Ohh, I'm really worried, scab!

RIZZO Okay, you bastard! *(*SHE *pushes him off bench and* THEY *fight on ground)*

ROGER and DOODY Fight! Fight! Yaaayy! *(Etc.)*

DANNY *(Separating them)* Come on, cut it out!

RIZZO *and* KENICKIE *stop fighting and glare at each other.*

Jesus, what a couple of fruitcakes!

RIZZO Well, he started it.

KENICKIE God, what a yo-yo! Make one little joke and she goes apeshit. *(*HE *sulks over to garbage can)*

DOODY Jeez, nice couple.

There is an uncomfortable pause onstage as the KIDS *hear* VINCE
FONTAINE *on radio.*

VINCE'S VOICE . . . 'cause tomorrow night yours truly, the Main
Brain, Vince Fontaine, will be M.C.ing the big dance bash out
at Rydell High School—in the boys' gym, and along with me
will be Mr. T.N.T. himself, Johnny Casino and the Gamblers.
So, make it a point to stop by the joint, Rydell High, 7:30
tomorrow night.

RIZZO Hey, Danny, you goin' to the dance tomorrow night?

DANNY I don't think so.

RIZZO Awww, you're all broke up over little Gidget!

DANNY Who?

RIZZO Ahh, c'mon, Zuko, why don'tcha take me to the dance—I
can pull that Sandra Dee crap, too. Right, you guys?

ROGER *and* DOODY *do MGM lion, and* RIZZO *sings "Look at me,
I'm Sandra Dee."*

RIZZO

Look at me, I'm Sandra Dee
Lousy with virginity.
Won't go to bed till I'm legally wed.
I can't, I'm Sandra Dee.

Watch it, hey, I'm Doris Day.
I was not brought up that way.
Won't come across, even Rock Hudson lost
His heart to Doris Day.

I don't drink or swear,
I don't rat my hair.

I get ill from one cigarette.
Keep your filthy paws off my silky drawers.
Would you pull that stuff with Annette?

SANDY *enters, hearing the last part of the song.* SONNY *is behind her.*

As for you, Troy Donahue,
I know what you wanna do.
You got your crust, I'm no object of lust.
I'm just plain Sandra Dee.
No, no, no, Sal Mineo,
I would never stoop so low.
Please keep your cool, now you're starting to drool, fongool!
I'm Sandra Dee!

SANDY *crosses to* RIZZO.

SONNY   Hey, Sandy, wait a minute . . . hey . . .

SANDY   *(To* RIZZO*)* Listen, just who do you think you are? I saw you making fun of me.

SANDY *leaps on* RIZZO *and the two* GIRLS *start fighting.* DANNY *pulls* SANDY *off.*

Let go of me! You dirty liar! Don't touch me!

SONNY *and* ROGER *hold* RIZZO.

RIZZO   Aaahh, let me go. I ain't gonna do nothin' to her. That chick's flipped her lid!

SANDY   *(To* DANNY*)* You tell them right now . . . that all those things you've been saying about me were lies. go on, tell 'em.

DANNY   Whattaya talkin' about? I never said anything about you.

SANDY   You creep! You think you're such a big man, don't ya? Trying to make me look like just another tramp.

RIZZO *charges at her. The* GUYS *hold* RIZZO *back.*

I don't know *why* I ever liked you, Danny Zuko.

SANDY *runs off in tears, stepping on* FRENCHY *'s fan magazine.* DANNY *starts after her, gives up.* FRENCHY *sadly picks up torn Ricky Nelson picture.*

DANNY   *(Turning to the* OTHERS*)* Weird chick! *(Pause)* Hey, Rizzo. You wanna go to the dance with me?

RIZZO   Huh? Yeah, sure. Why not?

ROGER   Hey, Jan. You got a date for the dance tomorrow night?

JAN   Tomorrow? Let me check. *(*SHE *takes out a little notebook and thumbs through it)* No, I don't. Why?

ROGER   You wanna go with me?

JAN   You kiddin' me? *(As* ROGER *shakes his head "no")* Yeah, sure, Roge!

DOODY   *(Moving to* FRENCHY*)* Hey, Frenchy, can you still go to the dance, now that you quit school?

FRENCHY   Yeah. I guess so. Why?

DOODY   Oh. Ahh, nothin'. . . . I'll see ya there.

SONNY   Hey, Kenickie, how 'bout givin' me a ride tomorrow, and I'll pick us up a couple a broads at the dance.

KENICKIE   Nah, I got a blind date from 'cross town. I hear she's a real bombshell.

MARTY   Gee, I don't even know if I'll go. All those silly kids.

DANNY   Okay, you can be the chaperone.

DOODY   *(Laughs)* Hey, Neat-o!

> DANNY *pinches* MARTY*'s* ass. MARTY *starts to chase* DANNY. ALL
> *sing "We Go Together."*

ALL

>We go together, like
>Rama-lama-lama, ka-dinga da ding-dong,
>Remembered forever, as
>Shoo-bop sha-wadda-wadda
>Yippity boom-de-boom
>Chang chang changitty-chang shoo-bop.
>That's the way it should be (Whaa-oohh! yeah!)
>
>We're one of a kind, like
>Dip-da-dip-da-dip
>Doo-wop da-dooby-doo.
>Our names are signed
>Boogedy, boogedy, boogedy, boogedy
>Shooby-doo-wop-she-bop
>Chang chang-a changitty-chang shoo-bop.
>We'll always be like one (Whaa-wha-wha-whaaaaaah)
>
>When we go out at night
>And stars are shining bright
>Up in the skies above,
>Or at the high school dance
>Where you can find romance
>Maybe it might be la-a-a-ah-ove
>
>We're for each other, like
>A-wop-baba-lu-mop and wop-bam-boom!
>Just like my brother, is

Sha-na-na-na-na-na yippity-dip-de-doom
Chang chang-a changitty-chang shoo-bop
We'll always be together!

At the end of the song, the lights fade on the KIDS *as* THEY *go off, laughing and horsing around, improvising various falsetto riffs.*

Over:
Costume sketch for
"Beauty School Dropout,"
Act II

*
GOWN
SHOWER
CURTAIN
WHITE ON
STRIPE

(chk pa
may b
bright

ACT II / SCENE 1

The GREASERS *run on and sing "Shakin' at the High School Hop." THEY are preparing for the high school dance—the* BOYS *combing hair, polishing shoes, etc., the* GIRLS *spraying hair, putting on crinolines, stuffing Kleenex into bras, etc.*

ALL

Well, honky-tonk baby, get on the floor.
All the cats are shoutin', they're yellin' for more.
My baby likes to rock, my baby likes to roll,
My baby does the chicken and she does the stroll:
Well, they shake it
Ohh, shake it
Yeah, shake it
Everybody shakin'
Shakin' at the high school hop.

DANNY Well, sock-hop baby,
GIRLS Roll up her crazy jeans.
GUYS Gonna rock to the music,
ALL Gonna dig the scene.
GIRLS Shimmy to the left,
GUYS Cha-cha to the right
ALL We gonna do the walk
Till broad daylight

Repeat Chorus

GIRLS Well, we're gonna alley-oop
On blueberry hill.
GUYS Hully gully with Lucille,
Won't be standin' still.
GIRLS Hand-jive baby,

ALL

Do the stomp with me.
I chalypso, do the slop,
Gonna bop with Mr. Lee.

Well, they shake it
Ohh, shake it
Yeah, shake it
Everybody's shakin'
Shakin' at the high school hop.

Instrumental chorus and dance while the GREASERS *move into the high school gym and are joined by* PATTY, EUGENE *and* MISS LYNCH, ALL *dancing wildly.*

Shake, rock and roll
Rock, roll and shake
Shake, rock and roll
Rock, roll and shake
Shake, rock and roll
Long live rock and roll.

Lights fade on dance and SANDY *is revealed in her bedroom.* SHE *turns up the volume on radio.*

ANNOUNCER   . . . continuing lovely dreamtime music on WLDL with a popular success from last summer: "It's Raining on Prom Night". . .

Song comes on radio. SANDY *sings lead vocal with the radio voice in harmony.*

RADIO VOICE

I was deprived of a young girl's dream
By the cruel force of nature from the blue.

SANDY and RADIO VOICE

Instead of a night full of romance supreme
All I got was a runny nose and Asiatic flu.

It's raining on prom night,
My hair is a mess.
It's running all over
My taffeta dress.
It's wilting the quilting in my Maidenform
And mascara flows right down my nose because of the storm.
I don't even have my corsage, oh gee
It fell down a sewer with my sister's I.D.

SANDY *talks verse while* RADIO VOICE *continues to sing.*

Yes, it's raining on prom night.
Oh, my darling, what can I do? I miss you.
It's raining rain from the skies
It's raining real tears from my eyes
Over you.

Dear God, let him feel the same way I do right now. Make him
    want to see me again! (SANDY *resumes singing the lead)*

Oh, what can I do?
It's raining rain from the skies,
It's raining tears from my eyes
Over you-ooo-ooo-ooo—rain-ing.

*After song, instrumental version of "Shakin' at the High School
Hop" continues. Lights fade out on* SANDY, *come up on the
high school dance. The couples are:* DANNY *and* RIZZO, JAN
and ROGER, FRENCHY *and* DOODY, PATTY *and* EUGENE. MISS
LYNCH *is overseeing the punchbowl.* MARTY *is alone and* SONNY
*is drinking from a half-pint in the corner. At the end of
"Shakin'," the* KIDS *cheer and yell.* JOHNNY CASINO, *with guitar*

on bandstand, introduces VINCE FONTAINE, *announcer for radio station* WAXX.

JOHNNY CASINO Hang loose, everybody. Here he is, the Main Brain —Vince Fontaine.

VINCE *(Dashes on and grabs mike)* I've had a lot of requests for a slow one. How 'bout it, Johnny Casino?

JOHNNY CASINO *(Grabbing mike)* Okay, Vince, here's a little number I wrote called "Enchanted Guitar."

VINCE *(Grabbing mike back)* And don't forget, only ten more minutes till the big Hand-Jive Contest.

Cheers and excited murmurs from the CROWD.

So, if you've got a steady get her ready.

JOHNNY CASINO *and the* BAND *do slow two-step instrumental as* VINCE *leaves bandstand and mills among* KIDS.

RIZZO Hey, Danny, you gonna be my partner for the dance contest?

DANNY Maybe, if nothing better comes along.

RIZZO Drop dead!

JAN *(Stumbling on* ROGER*'s feet)* Sorry.

ROGER Why don'tcha let *me* lead, for a change?

JAN I can't help it. I'm used to leading.

FRENCHY *(Dancing with* DOODY, *who is rocking back and forth in one spot)* Hey, Doody, can't you at least turn me around or somethin'?

DOODY Don't talk, I'm tryin' to count.

PATTY *dances near* DANNY *with* EUGENE, *who is pumping her arm vigorously.*

PATTY Danny, Danny!

DANNY Yeah, that's my name, don't wear it out.

PATTY How did the track tryouts go?

DANNY *(Nonchalantly)* I made the team.

PATTY Oh, wonderful! (SHE *starts signaling in pantomime for* DANNY *to cut in)*

RIZZO Hey, Zuko, I think she's tryin' to tell ya somethin'!

PATTY *'s pantomime becomes more desperate as* EUGENE *pumps harder.*

Go on, dance with her. You ain't doin' me no good.

DANNY *(Going up to* EUGENE*)* Hey, Euuu-gene, Betty Rizzo thinks you look like Pat Boone.

EUGENE Oh? (HE *walks over and stands near* RIZZO, *staring.* HE *polishes his white bucks on the back of his pants legs)*

DANNY *dances with* PATTY.

RIZZO Whataya say, fruit-boots?

EUGENE I understand you were asking about me?

RIZZO Yeah! I was wondering where you parked your hearse.

EUGENE *sits next to* RIZZO *as* RIZZO *offers him* SONNY *'s half-pint.*

SONNY *grabs it back.* PATTY *and* DANNY *are in a close dance clinch, not moving.*

PATTY   I never knew you were such a fabulous dancer, Danny. So sensuous and feline.

DANNY   Huh? Yeah?

Music tempo changes to cha-cha. KENICKIE *and* CHA-CHA DI GREGORIO *enter.*

CHA-CHA   God, nice time to get here. Look, the joint's half empty already.

KENICKIE   Ahh, knock it off! Can I help it if my car wouldn't start?

CHA-CHA   Jeez, what crummy decorations!

KENICKIE   Where'd ya think you were goin', American Bandstand?

CHA-CHA   We had a sock hop at St. Bernadette's once. The Sisters got real pumpkins and everything.

KENICKIE   Neat. They probably didn't have a bingo game that night. *(*HE *walks away and* CHA-CHA *trails behind him)*

VINCE   *(Coming up to* MARTY*)* Pardon me, weren't you a contestant in the Miss Rock 'n Roll Universe Pageant?

MARTY   Yeah, but I got disqualified 'cause I had a hickey on my neck.

The song ends and KIDS *cheer.* JOHNNY CASINO *looks for* VINCE FONTAINE *on the dance floor.*

JOHNNY CASINO   Hey, Vince . . . any more requests?

VINCE   *(Irritated, still looking at* MARTY. *Motions* JOHNNY *away with his hand)* Yeah, play anything!

JOHNNY CASINO   Okay, here's a little tune called "Anything."

Band plays instrumental stroll. MARTY, JAN *and* FRENCHY, VINCE, ROGER *and* DOODY *form facing lines as* DANNY *and* PATTY *come through center.*

PATTY   I can't imagine you ever having danced with Sandy like this.

DANNY   Whattaya mean?

PATTY   I mean her being so clumsy and all. She can't even twirl a baton right. In fact, I've been thinking of having a little talk with the coach about her.

DANNY   Why? Whatta you care?

PATTY   Well, I mean . . . even you have to admit she's a bit of a drip. I mean . . . isn't that why you broke up with her?

DANNY   Hey, listen . . . y'know she used to be a halfway decent chick before she got mixed up with you and your brown-nose friends.

DANNY walks away from her. PATTY, *stunned, runs to punch table.* KENICKIE *walks up to* RIZZO.

RIZZO   Hey, Kenickie, where ya been, the submarine races?

KENICKIE   Nah. I had to go to Egypt to pick up a date.

RIZZO   You feel like dancin'?

KENICKIE   Crazy. *(HE starts to dance off with* RIZZO*)*

EUGENE   It's been very nice talking to you, Betty.

RIZZO   Yeah, see ya around the bookmobile.

CHA-CHA moves to EUGENE, hoping EUGENE might ask her to dance, as band continues. SONNY gets up and crosses dance floor.

DOODY   *(Dropping out of the stroll line)* Hey, Rump, let's go have a weed.

ROGER   Yeah, okay.

JAN   Oh, Roger, would ya get me some punch?

ROGER   Whatsa matter? You crippled?

JAN sticks her tongue out at ROGER as he and DOODY start off. THEY bump into SONNY. The band plays a cha-cha.

VINCE   *(To MARTY)* I'm Vince Fontaine. Do your folks know I come into your room every night? Over WAXX, that is! I'm gonna judge the dance contest. Are you gonna be in it?

MARTY   I guess not. I ain't got a date.

VINCE   What? A knockout like you? Things sure have changed since I went to school . . . last year. Ha-Ha!

MARTY stares at him dumbly for a few seconds, then starts laughing. DOODY, SONNY, ROGER and DANNY are drinking and smoking in corner. CHA-CHA is dancing around EUGENE at bench.

DOODY   *(Pointing to CHA-CHA)* Hey, ain't that the chick Kenickie walked in with?

SONNY   Where?

DOODY   The one pickin' her nose over there.

SONNY   That's the baby.

ROGER Jesus, is she a gorilla!

SONNY I thought she was one of the steam-table ladies.

The GUYS *crack up.*

CHA-CHA *(To* EUGENE*)* Hey, did you come here to dance or didn't ya?

EUGENE Of course, but I never learned how to do this dance.

CHA-CHA Ahh, there's nothing to it. I'm gonna teach ballroom at the CYO. *(*SHE *grabs* EUGENE *in dance position)* Now, one-two-cha-cha-cha! Three-four-cha-cha-cha very-good-cha-cha-cha keep-it-up-cha-cha-cha . . .

EUGENE You certainly dance well.

CHA-CHA Thanks, ya can hold me a little tighter. I won't bite cha. *(*SHE *grabs* EUGENE *in a bear hug)*

Music ends, and KIDS *applaud.*

JOHNNY CASINO Thank you. This is Johnny Casino telling you when you hear the tone it will be exactly one minute to Hand-Jive Time!

Excited murmurs and scrambling for partners takes place on the dance floor as the band's guitarist makes a "twang" sound on his E string.

EUGENE *(To* CHA-CHA*)* Excuse me, it was nice meeting you.

CHA-CHA Hey, wait a minute . . . don'tcha want my phone number or somethin'?

EUGENE *(To* PATTY*)* Patty, you promised to be my partner for the dance contest, remember?

PATTY That's right. I almost forgot. *(SHE looks longingly toward DANNY as EUGENE pulls her away)*

DANNY *(Walking over to RIZZO and KENICKIE)* Hey, Rizzo. I'm ready to dance with you now.

RIZZO Don't strain yourself . . . I'm dancin' with Kenickie.

KENICKIE That's all right, Zuko, you can dance with my date. *(HE yells)* Hey, Charlene! C'mere.

CHA-CHA *(Walking over to KENICKIE)* Yeah, whattaya want?

KENICKIE How'dja like to dance this one with Danny Zuko?

CHA-CHA The big rod of the Burger Palace Boys? I didn't even know he saw me here.

DANNY *(Giving CHA-CHA a dismayed look)* I didn't.

CHA-CHA looks around in ecstasy.

JOHNNY Okay, alligators, here it is. The big one . . .

Drum roll.

The Hand-Jive Dance Contest. *(The KIDS cheer)* Let's get things under way by bringing up our own Miss Lynch.

The KIDS react. GUITAR PLAYER in band plays a few chords of "Rydell Fight Song" as MISS LYNCH comes up to the mike.

MISS LYNCH *(To JOHNNY CASINO)* Thank you, Clarence.

All the KIDS break up. JOHNNY CASINO mouths, "Fuck you, man" and gives KIDS "the finger."

Whenever you're finished. *(Noise subsides a little)* Before we

begin, I'd like to welcome you all to "Moonlight in the Tropics."
And I think we all owe a big round of applause to Patty Simcox
and her committee for the wonderful decorations.

Mixed reaction from CROWD.

CHA-CHA They shoulda got real coconuts!

MISS LYNCH Now, I'm sure you'll be glad to know that I'm not
judging this dance contest. *(A few* KIDS *cheer)* All right. All
right. I'd like to present Mr. Vince Fontaine. *(*KIDS *cheer, as* SHE
looks around) Mr. Fontaine?

VINCE *(Still with* MARTY, *yells)* Comin' right up! *(Aside to* MARTY
as HE *starts for the bandstand)* Stick around, cupcake. I'll be
right back.

MISS LYNCH As most of you know, Mr. Fontaine is an announcer
for radio station WAXX.

VINCE, *on the bandstand, whispers in her ear.*

Uh . . . *(Uncomfortably)* "Dig the scene on Big Fifteen." *(Cheer
goes up)* Now for the rules! One: All couples must be boy-girl.
Two: anyone using tasteless or vulgar movements will be disqualified. Three: If Mr. Fontaine taps you on the shoulder, you
must clear the dance floor immediately . . .

VINCE *(Grabbing the mike from* MISS LYNCH*)* I just wanna say, truly
in all sincerity, Miss Lynch, that you're doing a really, really
terrific job here, terrific. And I'll sure bet these kids are lucky
to have you for a teacher, 'cause I'll bet in all sincerity that you're
really terrific. *Is she terrific, kids? (The* KIDS *cheer)* Only thing
I wanna say, in all sincerity, is enjoy yourselves, have a ball,
'cause like we always say at Big Fifteen where the jocks hang out
—"If you're having fun, you're number one!" And some lucky
guy and gal is gonna go boppin' home with a stack of terrific
prizes. But don't feel bad if I bump yez out, 'cause it don't

matter if you win or lose, it's what ya do with those dancing shoes. So, okay, cats, throw your mittens around your kittens . . . and *away we go! (*VINCE *does Jackie Gleason pose)*

JOHNNY CASINO *sings "Born to Hand-Jive." During the dance,* COUPLES *are eliminated one by one as* VINCE FONTAINE *mills through the crowd, tapping each* COUPLE *and occasionally letting one of his hands slither down to rub one of the girls across the ass, or nonchalantly trying to "cop a feel."*

JOHNNY CASINO

Before I was born, late one night,
My papa said, "Everything's all right."
The doctor laughed, when ma laid down
With her stomach bouncin' all around
'Cause a be-bop stork was 'bout to arrive
And mama gave birth to the hand-jive!

I could barely walk when I milked a cow
And when I was three I pushed a plow.
While choppin' wood I'd move my legs
And started dancin' while I gathered eggs.
The townfolk clapped, I was only five,
He'll outdance 'em all, he's a born hand-jive!

Short guitar solo. Dance chorus.

Born to hand-jive, babeeeeeee!!
Born to hand-jive, baby!!

Dance chorus.

So I grew up dancin' on the stage,
Doin' the hand-jive became the rage.
But a jealous stud pulled a gun
And said "Let's see how fast you run."
Yeah, natural rhythm kept me alive
Out-dodgin' bullets with the ol' hand-jive!

Now, can you hand-jive, babeeeeeee??
Oh, can you hand-jive, baby?
Oh, yeah, oh, yeah, oh, yeah. Born to hand-jive!

Eventually, ALL *the* COUPLES *are eliminated except* DANNY *and* CHA-CHA. *On the final chorus, the* KIDS *stand around in a circle and clap in time.* VINCE FONTAINE *pulls* MISS LYNCH *onto the dance floor and tries to hog the spotlight from* DANNY *and* CHA-CHA. *At the end of the dance,* MISS LYNCH, *out of breath, returns to the bandstand,* VINCE FONTAINE *right behind her.*

MISS LYNCH   My goodness! Well, we have our winners. Will you step up here for your prizes? Daniel Zuko and . . . and . . .

DANNY *and* CHA-CHA, *swamped by the other* KIDS, *battle their way to the bandstand.*

CHA-CHA   Cha-Cha Di Gregorio.

MISS LYNCH   *(Taken aback at having to repeat the first name)* Uh . . . Cha-Cha Di Gregorio.

CHA-CHA   *(Grabbing mike)* They call me Cha-Cha 'cause I'm the best dancer at St. Bernadette's.

Mixed reaction and ad libs from CROWD.

MISS LYNCH   Oh . . . that's very nice. Congratulations to both of you, and here are your prizes: Two record albums, "Hits from the House of WAXX," autographed by Mr. Vince Fontaine. *(*SHE *holds up album with large letters* WAXX. KIDS *cheer)* Two free passes to the Twi-Light Drive-In Theater . . . good on any week night. *(*KIDS *cheer)* A coupon worth ten dollars off at Robert Hall. *(*KIDS *boo)* And last but not least, your trophies, prepared by Mrs. Schneider's art class. *(Cheers and applause.* MISS LYNCH *presents* DANNY *and* CHA-CHA *with two hideous ceramic nebbishes in dance positions, mounted on blocks of wood)*

VINCE   *(Grabbing the mike from* MISS LYNCH*)* Weren't they terrific?

C'mon, let's hear it for these kids! *(KIDS cheer)* Only thing I wanna say before we wrap things up is that you kids at Rydell are the greatest!

KENICKIE   Fuckin' A!

VINCE   Last dance, ladies' choice.

Band plays slow instrumental. DANNY *takes record album from* CHA-CHA, *giving her his trophy in exchange and exits.* COUPLES *leave dance, one by one, until* CHA-CHA *is left alone.* PATTY, EUGENE *and* MISS LYNCH *clean up after dance.* EACH *exits as the lights change to new scene.*

SCENE 2

It is evening a few days later in front of the Burger Palace. FRENCHY *is pacing around, magazine in hand, looking at sign on Burger Palace window: "Counter Girl Wanted." After a few moments* SONNY, KENICKIE *and* DOODY *enter with weapons:* DOODY *with a baseball bat,* SONNY *with a zip gun,* KENICKIE *with a lead pipe and chain.* THEY *wear leather jackets and engineer boots.*

KENICKIE   Hey, Sonny, what Cracker Jack box ja' get that zip gun out of, anyway?

SONNY   What do ya mean, I made it in shop. *(Seeing FRENCHY)* Hey, what's shakin', French? You get out of beauty school already?

FRENCHY   Oh . . . I cut tonight. Those beauty teachers they got working there don't know nothin'. Hey, what's with the arsenal?

DOODY   We gotta rumble with the Flaming Dukes.

FRENCHY   No lie! How come?

KENICKIE   Remember that scurvy broad I took to the dance?

FRENCHY *looks blank.*

DOODY   *(Helpfully)* Godzilla!

DOODY and KENICKIE   *(*THEY *do imitation of* CHA-CHA *and* EUGENE *dancing)* "One-two-cha-cha-cha!"

FRENCHY   Oh! Y'mean Cha-Cha Dee Garage-io . . . the one Danny won the dance contest with?

SONNY   Well, it turns out she goes steady with the leader of the Flaming Dukes. And she told this guy Danny got in her silks.

KENICKIE   If he did, he musta been makin' a bug collection for Biology.

ALL GUYS *laugh.* KENICKIE *joins in, laughing at his own joke.* DANNY *enters jogging, wearing a white track suit with a brown and green number four on his back. The trunks are white with a thin green and brown stripe running vertically on each side.* HE *has a relay-race baton.*

FRENCHY   *(Seeing* DANNY*)* Hey look . . . ain't that Danny?

DOODY   Hey, Danny!

FRENCHY   What's he doing in his underwear?

DOODY   That's a track suit! Hiya, Danny.

DANNY *stops.* HE*'s panting.* GUYS *gather around him.*

KENICKIE   Jesus, Zuko, where do you keep your Wheaties?

DANNY   *(Reaching in front of jock strap and pulling out a crumpled pack of Luckies)* Ha-ha. Big joke. *(*HE *lights a cigarette)*

SONNY   Hey, it's a good thing you're here. We're supposed to rumble the Dukes tonight!

DANNY   *(Alarmed)* What time?

KENICKIE   Nine o'clock.

DANNY   *(Annoyed)* Nice play! I got field training till 9:30.

KENICKIE   Can't ya sneak away, man?

DANNY   Not a chance! The coach'd kick my ass.

SONNY   The coach!

DANNY   Besides, what am I supposed to do, stomp on somebody's face with my gym shoes? *(HE puts cigarettes back in jock)*

KENICKIE   Ahh, c'mon, Zuko, whattaya tryin' to prove with this track team crap!?

DANNY   Why? Whatta you care? Look, I gotta cut. I'm in the middle of a race right now. See ya later.

SONNY   You got the hots for that cheerleader or somethin'?

DANNY   How'd you like a fat lip, Sonny? Nine o'clock, huh? I'll be back if I can get away. Later! *(Silence.* DANNY *stands glaring at the* GUYS *for a moment and then* HE *runs off, cigarette in his mouth)*

SONNY   Neat guy, causes a ruckus and then he cuts out on us!

KENICKIE   Jeez, next thing ya know he'll be gettin' a crew cut!

DOODY   He'd look neater with a flat top.

KENICKIE   C'mon, let's go eat. *(HE and* SONNY *start toward Burger Palace)*

SONNY Hey, Kenicks, you wanna split a superburger?

KENICKIE Yeah. All right.

SONNY Good. Lend me a half a buck.

SONNY *and* KENICKIE *exit into Burger Palace, stashing their weapons in a painted oil drum used for garbage.*

DOODY Hey, Frenchy, maybe I'll come down to your beauty school some night this week . . . we can have a Coke or somethin'.

FRENCHY *(Uncertain)* Yeah . . . yeah, sure.

DOODY *smiles and, depositing his baseball hat in the same oil drum, exits into the Burger Palace.*

(To her movie magazine) Jeez! What am I gonna do? I mean, I can't just tell everybody I dropped out of beauty school. I can't go in the Palace for a job . . . with all the guys sittin' around. Boy, I wish I had one of those Guardian Angel things like in that Debbie Reynolds movie. Would that be neat . . . somebody always there to tell ya what's the best thing to do.

Spooky angelic guitar chords. FRENCHY*'s Guardian* TEEN ANGEL *appears.* HE *is a Fabian-like rock singer. White Fabian sweater with the collar turned up, white chinos, white boots, a large white comb sticking out of his pocket.* HE *sings "Beauty School Dropout." After the first verse, a chorus of* ANGELS *appears: a group of* GIRLS *in white plastic sheets with their hair in white plastic rollers, arranged in a halo effect.* THEY *provide background doo-wahs.*

TEEN ANGEL

Your story's sad to tell:
A teenage ne'er-do-well,
Most mixed-up non-delinquent on the block,
Your future's so unclear now.

What's left of your career now?
Can't even get a trade-in on your smock.
(ANGEL CHORUS *enters*)

Beauty school dropout,
No graduation day for you.
Beauty school dropout,
Missed your midterms and flunked shampoo.
Well, at least you could have taken time
To wash and clean your clothes up
After spending all that dough to have
The doctor fix your nose up.
Baby, get movin',
Why keep your feeble hopes alive?
What are you provin'?
You got the dream but not the drive.
If you go for your diploma you could join a steno pool
Turn in your teasing comb and go back to high school.

Beauty school dropout,
Hangin' around the corner store.
Beauty school dropout,
It's about time you knew the score.
Well, they couldn't teach you anything,
You think you're such a looker,
But no customer would go to you
Unless she was a hooker.
Baby, don't sweat it,
You're not cut out to hold a job.
Better forget it,
Who wants their hair done by a slob?
Now your bangs are curled, your lashes twirled,
But still the world is cruel.
Wipe off that angel face and go back to high school.

At the end of the stanza the TEEN ANGEL *hands* FRENCHY *a high
school diploma, which* SHE *uncurls, looks at, crumples up and
throws away. The* TEEN ANGEL *and* CHOIR *look on.* FRENCHY
walks away.

Baby, ya blew it.
You put our good advice to shame.
How could you do it?
Betcha Dear Abby'd say the same.
Guess there's no way to get through to you,
No matter who may try.
Might as well go back to that malt shop in the sky.

The TEEN ANGEL *and* CHOIR *exit.* DOODY, KENICKIE *and* SONNY *come out of Burger Palace as the place is closing. The* GUYS *retrieve their weapons from the trash can.*

SONNY   Looks like they ain't gonna show. They said they'd be here at nine.

DOODY   What time is it?

SONNY   *(Looking at his watch)* Hey man, it's almost five after. C'mon, let's haul ass.

KENICKIE   Give 'em another ten minutes. Hey, what the hell happened to Rump?

SONNY   Who cares about lard-ass. Who'da ever thought Zuko'd punk out on us.

KENICKIE   Nice rumble! A herd of Flaming Dukes against you, me and Howdy Doody.

DOODY   Hey, I heard about this one time when the Dukes pulled a sneak attack by drivin' up in a stolen laundry truck. That really musta been cool.

SONNY   *(Suddenly)* Hey, you guys, watch out for a fuckin' laundry truck.

SONNY *and* KENICKIE *tense up, looking around.* DOODY *stares blankly.* ROGER *comes charging on in a frenzy with a car antenna in his hand.*

ROGER   *(Shouting)* Okay, where the fuck are they? *(Looking around)* Hey, where's Zuko?

SONNY   Well, look who's here. Where you been, chub-nuts?

ROGER   Hey, bite the weenie, moron. My old man made me help him paint the goddamned basement. I couldn't even find my bullwhip. I had to bust off an aerial.

SONNY   Ha, whattaya expect to do with that thing?

KENICKIE   *(Grabbing* ROGER*'s antenna and imitating a newscaster)* This is Dennis James bringing you the play-by-play of Championship Gangfighting!

ROGER   *(Grabbing antenna back)* Hey, listen, I'll take this over any of *those* Tinker Toys!

KENICKIE   Oh, yeah? Okay, Rump, how 'bout if I hit ya over the head with that thing and then I hit ya over the head with my lead pipe and ya can tell me which one hurts more—okay?

ROGER   Okay. C'mon and get it! C'mon, Kenickie! *(*HE *holds out the antenna. As* KENICKIE *reaches for it* HE *lashes the air above* KENICKIE*'s head and almost hits* SONNY *behind him)*

SONNY   Hey, watch it with that thing, pimple-puss!

ROGER   Hey, whatsamatter, LaTierri, afraid ya might get hurt a little?

SONNY   Listen, chickenshit, you're gonna look real funny cruisin' around the neighborhood in a wheelchair.

ROGER   Well, why don'tcha use that thing, then? You got enough rubber bands there to start three paper routes.

KENICKIE   *(Grabbing* DOODY*'s baseball bat)* Hey, Rump! C'mon, let's see ya try that again.

ROGER   What'sa matter, Kenicks? What happened to your big bad pipe?

SONNY, DOODY, KENICKIE *and* ROGER *begin circling.* KENICKIE *knocks antenna out of* ROGER*'s hand with bat.* KENICKIE *and* SONNY *close in on* ROGER, *now defenseless.*

KENICKIE   Okay, Rump, how's about mooning the Flaming Dukes? Pants 'em!

SONNY *and* KENICKIE *leap on* ROGER *and get his pants off.* DOODY *helps with the shoes.* SONNY *and* KENICKIE *run off with* ROGER*'s pants as* DOODY *gathers up weapons.*

DOODY   Hey, you guys, wait up! *(*HE *starts to run off, goes back to hand* ROGER *his antenna, then exits)*

ROGER   Oh shit! *(*HE *stands a moment, bewildered, holding antenna, then exits, disgusted)*

SCENE 3

Lights come up on Greased Lightning at the Twi-Light Drive-In Theater. SANDY *and* DANNY *are sitting alone at opposite ends of the front seat staring straight ahead in awkward silence. Movie music is coming out of a portable speaker.* DANNY *is sipping a quart of beer. Dialogue from the movie begins to come out of the speaker.*

GIRL'S VOICE   It was . . . like an animal . . . with awful clawing hands and . . . and . . . hideous fangs. Oh, it was like a nightmare!

HERO'S VOICE   There, there, you're safe now, Sheila.

SCIENTIST'S VOICE   Poor Todd. The radiation has caused him to mutate. He's become half-man, half-monster . . . like a werewolf.

SHEILA'S VOICE   But, doctor . . . he . . . he's my *brother*. And his big stock car race is tomorrow!

A werewolf cry is heard.

HERO'S VOICE   Great Scott! It's a full moon!

Silence. DANNY *stretches, puts arm across* SANDY*'s shoulder.* HE *tries to get arm around her.* SHE *moves away.*

DANNY   Why don'tcha move over a little closer? *(Removes his arm from the back of the seat)*

SANDY   This is all right.

DANNY   Well, can't ya at least smile or somethin'? Look, Sandy, I practically had to bust Kenickie's arm to get his car for tonight. The guys are really p.o.'d at me. I mean, I thought we were gonna forget all about that scene in the park with Sonny and Rizzo and everything. I told ya on the phone I was sorry.

SANDY   I know you did.

DANNY   Well, you believe me, don't ya?

SANDY   I guess so. It's just that everything was so much easier when there was just the two of us.

DANNY   Yeah, I know . . . but . . . *(Suddenly)* Hey, you ain't goin' with another guy, are ya?

SANDY   No. Why?

DANNY *(Trying to take off his high school ring)* Err . . . oh, ah . . . nothin'. Well, yeah . . . uh . . . ahhh, shit! I was gonna ask ya to take my ring. *(HE finally holds out the ring)*

SANDY Oh, Danny. I don't know what to say.

DANNY Well, don'tcha want it?

SANDY *(Smiles shyly)* Uh-huh.

DANNY *puts ring on* SANDY*'s finger.* SHE *kisses him lightly.*

DANNY I shoulda gave it to ya a long time ago.

THEY *kiss.*

I really like you, Sandy.

THEY *kiss again,* DANNY *getting more aggressive and passionate as the kiss goes on.*

SANDY Danny, take it easy! What are you trying to do? *(SHE squirms away from him)*

DANNY Whatsa' matter?

SANDY Well, I mean . . . I thought we were just gonna—you know —be steadies.

DANNY Well, whattaya' think goin' steady is, anyway? *(HE grabs her again)* C'mon, Sandy!

SANDY Stop it! I've never seen you like this.

DANNY Relax, willya, nobody's watchin' us!

SANDY Danny, please, you're hurting me.

DANNY *lets go and* SANDY *breaks away.*

DANNY   Whattaya' gettin' so shook up about? I thought I meant somethin' to ya.

SANDY   You do. But I'm still the same girl I was last summer. Just because you give me your ring doesn't mean we're gonna go all the way. (SHE *opens the car door and gets out*)

DANNY   Hey, Sandy, wait a minute.

SANDY *slams car door on* DANNY*'s hand.* HE *howls in pain.*

SANDY   I'm sorry, Danny. Maybe we better just forget about it. (SHE *gives* DANNY *his ring back. When* HE *refuses,* SHE *leaves it on the car hood and exits*)

DANNY   Hey, Sandy, where you goin'? You can't just walk out of a drive-in!

Movie VOICES *are heard again.*

HERO'S VOICE   Look, Sheila! The full moon is sinking behind "Dead Man's Curve."

DANNY *gets out of car to get the ring.*

SHEILA'S VOICE   Yes, Lance . . . and with it . . . all our dreams.

Werewolf howl. DANNY *sings "Alone at a Drive-In Movie," with werewolf howls coming from movie and the* BURGER PALACE BOYS *singing background "doo-wops" in* DANNY*'s mind.*

DANNY

> I'm all alone
> At the drive-in movie.
> It's a feelin' that ain't too groovy,
> Watchin' werewolves without you.

Offstage wolf howl.

Gee, it's no fun
Drinkin' beer in the back seat.
All alone just ain't too neat
At the passion pit, wanting you.

And when the intermission elf
Moves the clock's hands
While he's eating everything
Sold at the stand.

DANNY *gets into car.*

When there's one minute to go
Till the lights go down low,
I'll be holding the speaker knobs
Missing you so.

I can't believe it,
Unsteamed windows I can see through.
Might as well be in an igloo
'Cause the heater doesn't work . . .
As good as you.

Lights fade on DANNY *as* HE *drives off in car.*

SCENE 4

A party in JAN's *basement.* ROGER *and* DOODY *are sitting on
barstools singing "Rock 'n Roll Party Queen" accompanied by*
DOODY's *guitar.* KENICKIE *and* RIZZO *are dancing.* SONNY *and*
MARTY *are on couch tapping feet and drinking beer.* FRENCHY
is sitting on floor next to record player keeping time to the music.
JAN *is swaying to the music.* SANDY *sits alone on stairs trying to
fit in and enjoy herself.* DANNY *is not present.*

DOODY and ROGER

> Little girl—y'know who I mean—
> Pretty soon she'll be seventeen.
> They tell me her name's Betty Jean,
> The-ha-ha rock 'n roll party queen.
>
> Friday night and she's got a date.
> Goin' places—just a-stayin' out late,
> Droppin' dimes in the record machine.
> Ah-ho-ho, rock 'n roll party queen.
>
> Pa-pa-pa-pa-pa oh no,
> Can I have the car tonight?
> Bay-ba, bay-bee, can I be the one
> To love you with all my might (I-yi-yi-yi-)
>
> She's the girl that all the kids know,
> Talk about her wherever she goes.
> I could write a fan magazine
> About that rock 'n roll party queen.
>
> Bomp-ba bomp-ba-bomp, you should see her
> Shake to the latest dance.
> Bay-ba bay-bee, no, don't call it puppy love,
> Don'tcha wanna true romance? (I-yi-yi-yi)
>
> Oh rockin' and-a rollin' little party queen.
> We gonna do the stroll, hey, party queen.
> Know I love you so, my party queen,
> You're my rockin' and my rollin'
> Party quee-een!

SANDY   Don't put too many records on, Frenchy. I'm going to leave
in a couple of minutes.

KENICKIE   Aahh, come on! You ain't takin' your record player already! The party's just gettin' started.

RIZZO *(Moving to* SANDY *at steps)* Yeah, she's cuttin' out 'cause Zuko ain't here.

SANDY No, I'm not! I didn't come here to see him.

RIZZO No? What'dja come for, then?

SANDY Uh . . . because I was invited.

RIZZO We only invited ya 'cause we needed a record player.

JAN *(Trying to avoid trouble, motions* FRENCHY *to come out to the kitchen)* Hey, French!

FRENCHY *(Putting her hand on* SANDY*'s arm)* Don't mind her, Sandy. C'mon, let's go help Jan fix the food.

The GUYS *all gather together at the couch looking at a View Master.*

MARTY *(Moving to* RIZZO, *who is sitting alone on steps)* Jesus, you're really a barrel of laughs tonight, Rizzo. You havin' your friend?

RIZZO Huh?

MARTY Your friend. Your period.

RIZZO Don't I wish! I'm about five days late.

MARTY You think maybe you're p.g.?

RIZZO I don't know—big deal.

MARTY How'd you let a thing like that happen anyway?

RIZZO It wasn't my fault. The guy was usin' a thing, but it broke.

MARTY Holy cow!

RIZZO Yeah. He got it in a machine at a gas station. Y'know, one of those four for a quarter jobs.

MARTY Jeez, what a cheapskate!

KENICKIE *walks past them to get a can of beer.*

Hey, it's not Kenickie, is it?

RIZZO Nah! You don't know the guy.

MARTY Aahh, they're all the same! Ya remember that disc jockey I met at the dance? I caught him puttin' aspirin in my Coke.

RIZZO Hey, promise you won't tell anybody, huh?

MARTY Sure, I won't say nothin'.

RIZZO *(Moves to* GUYS *at couch)* Hey, what happened to the music? Why don't you guys sing another song?

ROGER Okay. Hey, Dude, let's do that new one by the Tinkletones?

JAN, FRENCHY *and* SANDY *enter to hear song.*

DOODY and ROGER

Each night I cry myself to sleep,
The girl I love is gone for keeps.
Ooo-wa ooo-ooo-wa. . . .

During the song, MARTY *whispers to* KENICKIE, *who angrily goes over to* RIZZO.

KENICKIE Hey, Rizzo, I hear you're knocked up.

Song stops.

RIZZO *(Glaring at* MARTY*)* You do, huh? Boy, good news really travels fast!

KENICKIE Hey, listen, why didn't you tell me?

RIZZO Don't worry about it, Kenickie. You don't even know who the guy is.

KENICKIE Huh? Thanks a lot, kid.

HE *walks away, hurt, leaves the party. The* GROUP *urges him to stay.* RIZZO, *upset, sits looking after him.*

SONNY *(Coming over to* RIZZO*)* Hey, Rizz, how's tricks? Look, if you ever need somebody to talk to . . .

RIZZO You think you can get a little without usin' a safety, right? Get lost, Sonny.

DOODY Tough luck, Rizzo.

ROGER Listen, Rizz, I'll help you out with some money if you need it.

RIZZO Forget it, I don't want any handouts.

FRENCHY It ain't so bad, Rizz—you get to stay home from school.

JAN Hey, you want to stay over tonight, Rizz?

RIZZO Hey, why don't you guys just flake off and leave me alone?

There is an awkward silence.

JAN It's getting late, anyway—I guess it might be better if everybody went home. C'mon, let's go!

JAN *gives* SONNY *a push.* DOODY *and* FRENCHY *exit.*

MARTY   Hey, French . . . wait up!

MARTY *gets her purse, which is near* RIZZO; SHE *avoids eye contact.* RIZZO *glares viciously at her.*

ROGER   See ya, Rizz. *(Looks at* RIZZO *a moment and exits)*

SONNY   *(To* JAN*)* Tell her I didn't mean anything, will ya? *(Exits)*

RIZZO *begins to clean up.*

JAN   Just leave that stuff, Rizzo. I'll get it.

RIZZO   Look, it's no bother. I don't mind.

JAN *exits.*

SANDY   *(Collecting her record player and purse)* I'm sorry to hear you're in trouble, Rizzo.

RIZZO   Bullshit! What are you gonna do—give me a whole sermon about it?

SANDY   No. But doesn't it bother you that you're pregnant?

RIZZO   Look, that's my business. It's nobody else's problem.

SANDY   Do you really believe that? Didn't you see Kenickie's face when he left here?

RIZZO *turns away.*

It's Kenickie, isn't it? *(Awkward pause)* Well, I guess I've said too much already. Good luck, Rizzo. *(*SHE *starts to leave)*

RIZZO   *(Turns and glares at her)* Just a minute, Miss Tight-Ass! Who do you think you are? Handing me all this sympathy crap! Since you know all the answers, how come I didn't see Zuko here tonight? You just listen to me, Miss Sandra Dee. *(Sings "There Are Worse Things I Could Do")*

There are worse things I could do
Than go with a boy or two,
Even though the neighborhood
Thinks I'm trashy and no good.
I suppose it could be true
But there's worse things I could do.

I could flirt with all the guys,
Smile at them and bat my eyes,
Press against them when we dance
Make them think they stand a chance,
Then refuse to see it through.
That's a thing I'd never do.

I could stay home every night,
Wait around for Mister Right,
Take cold showers every day,
And throw my life away
For a dream that won't come true.

I could hurt someone like me
Out of spite or jealousy.
I don't steal and I don't lie,
But I can feel and I can cry,
A fact I'll bet you never knew,
But to cry in front of you—
That's the worst thing I could do.

Lights fade out on RIZZO *as* SANDY *exits in tears carrying her record player.* SHE *goes into her bedroom and sits down on her bed, dejectedly.* SHE *sings a reprise of "Look at me, I'm Sandra Dee."*

SANDY

Look at me, there has to be
Something more than what they see.
Wholesome and pure, also scared and unsure,
A poor man's Sandra Dee.
When they criticize and make fun of me,
Can't they see the tears in my smile?
Don't they realize there's just one of me
And it has to last me a while?

(SHE *picks up the phone and dials)* Hello, Frenchy? Can you
come over for a while? And bring your makeup case. (SHE *hangs
up)*

Sandy, you must start anew.
Don't you know what you must do?
Hold your head high,
Take a deep breath and cry
Goodbye
To Sandra Dee.

On last line of song SHE *reaches for Kleenex and stuffs tissues into
her bra. Lights fade.*

SCENE 5

Lights come up on the inside of the Burger Palace. ROGER,
DOODY, KENICKIE *and* SONNY *are sitting at counter.*

ROGER   Hey, you guys wanta come over to my house to watch the
Mickey Mouse Club?

PATTY *enters in cheerleader costume, dragging pom-poms dispir-
itedly.*

Hey, whattaya say, Mary Hartline?

PATTY *ignores them.*

SONNY *(Loudly)* She ain't talkin'.

DOODY Maybe she had a fight with Danny.

KENICKIE Hey, jugs! Why don't ya make me a track star too?

SONNY Nah, get *me* out on that field. I'm a better broad jumper than Zuko.

The GUYS *laugh.*

PATTY *(Turning on them)* You're disgusting, all of you! You can *have* your Danny Zuko, you worthless bums.

ROGER Nice talk!

DOODY Whatsa matter? Don't you like Danny anymore?

PATTY As if you didn't know. He quit the track team!

GUYS Huh?

PATTY I just found out. The other day the coach asked Danny, perfectly nicely, to try to get to practice on time. Danny made a shamefully crass gesture and walked off the field.

SONNY He gave him the finger!

GUYS *crack up.*

ROGER What a neat!

PATTY Not only that, before he left the locker room, he . . . he . . . smeared Ben-Gay in the team captain's athletic supporter.

The GUYS *double up.* DANNY *enters. The* GUYS *immediately crowd around him.*

DANNY   Hey, you guys!

KENICKIE   Hey, Zuko!

SONNY   Whattaya say, Zuke? Where ya been?

DOODY   Hi, Danny.

DANNY *stands open-mouthed, bewildered by all the sudden attention.* PATTY *looks on disapprovingly.*

DANNY   I guess you got the word, huh?

ROGER   Hey, come on, we were just goin' over to my house to watch Mickey Mouse Club.

DANNY   *(Enthusiastically)* Yeah?

PATTY   Danny! I want to talk to you.

DANNY *motions to* GUYS *to be cool for a second as* HE *crosses to* PATTY.

DANNY   Ease off, Patty!

PATTY   *(Dagger eyes)* It's very *important*, Danny!

GUYS *all crowd around* DANNY *again.*

SONNY   Aahh, come on, Zuko! It'll be neat. Annette's startin' to get big knockers!

DANNY   *(Smiles)* Solid! Later, Patty.

GUYS *start to leave.* MARTY, FRENCHY, RIZZO *and* JAN *in Pink*

Ladies jackets enter silently, gesturing the GUYS *to be cool as* THEY *take up defiant positions.* SANDY *enters, now a Greaser's dream girl. A wild new hair style, black leather motorcycle jacket, skin-tight slacks, gold hoop earrings. Yet* SHE *actually looks prettier and more alive than* SHE *ever has.* SHE *is chewing gum and smoking a cigarette.* SHE *slouches casually and French inhales.*

RIZZO   *(Aside to* SANDY*)* Remember, play it cool.

DANNY   *(Turns and sees* SANDY*)* Hey Sandy! Wow, what a total! Wick-*ed!*

SANDY   *(Tough and cool)* What's it to ya, Zuko?

DANNY   Hey, we was just goin' to check out The Mouseketeers. How would you like to come along?

PATTY   Danny, what's gotten into you? You couldn't possibly be interested in that . . . that floozy.

SANDY *looks to* RIZZO *for her next move. Then* SHE *strolls over to* PATTY, *studies her calmly, and punches her in the eye.* PATTY *falls.*

GIRLS   *Yaa-aay!*

PATTY   Oh, my God, I'm going to have a black eye! *(*SHE *bawls)*

FRENCHY   *(Opening purse)* Don't sweat it. I'll fix it up. I just got a job demonstrating this new miracle makeup at Woolworth's.

DANNY   Hey, Sandy, you're somethin' else!

SANDY   Oh, so ya noticed, huh? *(*SHE *looks him calmly in the eye and walks coolly over to microphone, picks it up, walks back to* DANNY. SHE *makes a classic gesture: Right hand strikes left inner elbow; left forearm swings up, mike in hand. Better known as an "up yours" gesture)* Tell me about it, stud!

DANNY *(Sings "All Choked Up."* BURGER PALACE BOYS *join in, doing background)*

Well, I feel so strange, well, upon my word.
Now my brain is reeling and my eyesight's blurred,
I tremble a lot,
I'm nervous and hot,
Uh-huh! I'm all choked up.

There's a fire alarm wailin' in my head,
And my circulation says "Condition Red."
I'm in a cold sweat,
My T-shirt's all wet,
Uh-huh! I'm all choked up.

Oh, baby, baby, baby,
Take my heart before it breaks.
My knees are weak, my backbone quakes,
My hands are colder than ice,
My throat's locked in a vise.
Come on and change my pain to paradise.

There's a fever runnin' through my skin.
Can'tcha hear me knockin', won'tcha let me in?
You know I'm your fool,
Now don'tcha be cruel.
Uh huh! I'm all choked up.

GIRLS Now, listen here:

SANDY

So you're spinnin' round in a dizzy spell,
It's a situation I know pretty well.
Yeah, I've been there too
So I feel for you
Uh-huh! I'm all choked up

GIRLS And furthermore:

SANDY

So you're down and out, you're against a wall,
And you're sayin' I'm the one that did it all.
I'm sure you're sincere,
It gets me right here.
Uh-huh! I'm all choked up!

Oh, baby, take it slow and don't complain.
My poor heart just can't stand the strain.
Hey, I can cure your disease.
Let's hear you say "Pretty please",
And take your medicine down on your knees!

DANNY and GUYS

Got a fever, a hundred four Fahrenheit.
Need your lovin', can I come over tonight?
Feelin' lowdown, my equilibrium's shot,
Gimme, gimme, that tranquilizer you got.

DANNY	Oh, baby, take my ring 'Cause you're my match.
SANDY	Well, I still think There's strings attached.
DANNY	You're writin' my epitaph.
SANDY	Well, that's just tough and a half.
DANNY	You're gonna make me die!
SANDY	Don't make me laugh!

DANNY and SANDY

Well, I might forgive what you put me through,
'Cause I do believe you really love me too.
I look in your eyes,

The suffering dies.
Uh, huh! I'm all choked up.

ALL

Hey, hey, hey, hey,
I'm all choked up.
Hey, Hey, hey, hey.

DANNY and SANDY   *(To a "Hum shoo-bee doo-wop" background by the OTHERS)*

I'm all choked up
Uh-huh!
Uh-huh!

ALL

Ow!

DANNY   Hey, I still got my ring! I guess you're still kinda mad at me, huh? *(HE holds out his ring)*

SANDY   Nah. Fuck it!

THEY *kiss and hug quickly.*

ROGER   Hey, we just gonna stand around here all day? Let's get outta here!

DOODY   Yeah, we're missin' "Anything-Can-Happen" Day! *(HE pairs off with FRENCHY)*

DANNY   Yeah, let's cut! You comin', Big D?

SANDY   Solid! Hey, Patty, you wanna come?

PATTY   Oh. Well, thanks, but I wouldn't want to be in the way.

SANDY   Nah. It don't matter. Right?

DANNY   Hell, no. C'mon, Patty!

PATTY crosses up to door near DANNY.

SONNY   *(Goes over to MARTY)* Hey, Marty, did I tell ya I'm gettin'
a new Impala?

MARTY   Ohh, would you paint my name on it?

*SONNY nods "sure" and puts arm around her. THEY head for door
area.*

RIZZO   *(Crossing to KENICKIE)* Hey, Kenickie, can we stop at the
drugstore? I think I'm getting my friend.

*KENICKIE puts arm around her as all KIDS smile and cheer for
RIZZO.*

FRENCHY   Gee, the whole crowd's together again. I could cry.

JAN   Gee, me too!

SANDY   Yeah, I'm all choked up.

*The KIDS all have their arms around each other as THEY sing a
one-verse reprise of "We Go Together" and go off dancing and
singing.*

WARREN CASEY grew up in Yonkers, New York, and attended Syracuse University. During the "grease" period of the late 50's, he learned a lot about the teenagers of the time while working as a teacher in upstate New York. He also became active in local little theater groups. In the early 60's he moved to Chicago, where he worked as a record salesman and as assistant manager of a chain of corset shops. Meanwhile he continued acting, appearing in about thirty shows in Chicago community theaters. He taught himself how to play the guitar and began writing songs for the amusement of himself and his friends. *Grease* was his first attempt at writing a show. He is now working on a projected musical biography of the late-19th-century showmen Harrigan and Hart.

JIM JACOBS was born and raised in Chicago where during the Golden Era of rock 'n roll (1956–1960) he was a "greaser" at Taft High School, where he played guitar and sang with such illustrious groups as D.D.T. and The Dynamiters, and Lefty and The El-Rays. His curiosity about music soon had him sneaking into the "hot spots" of Chicago's South Side and going to the Maxwell Street area where he learned to play blues by "sitting in" with such legendary street singers and blues artists as Blind Arvella Grey, Little Walter, Daddy Stovepipe and Blind Jim Brewer. Around 1963 he became involved with a local theater group, where he met Warren Casey. During the next five years he worked with Paul Sills and appeared in over fifty community theater productions around Chicago while employed as a writer during the day. Professionally he has worked both as an actor and writer for theater, films, recordings and commercials. His title role in the Midwest premiere of *Jimmy Shine* got him a nomination for Chicago's Best Actor of the Year. Most recently, he appeared on Broadway in the Pulitzer Prize-winning *No Place To Be Somebody*.